Testimonials

"Investing in my culture through Culture Fulfillment produced the highest return for a low investment, and was one of the best things I could have done for the company. Implementing Will's program got it done, and we continue to enjoy double-digit growth." —*David Nance, CEO, SABRE.*

"Ink Factory's Values emerged thanks to a great working session hosted by Will Scott for our entire team. We gathered together to discuss, consolidate, and prioritize our three core values - and Will played an important role in those discussions."—*Dusty Folwarczny, Co-Founder + CEO, Ink Factory.*

"Working with Will has helped propel our business. Culture Fulfillment helped us define, refine, and visualize our core values, our purpose, and our workflows. From how we communicate to the deep detail of the numbers we track, the ROI of working on our culture has been off the charts." —*Chris Madden, Co-Founder, Matchnode.*

"Working with Will Scott's Culture Fulfillment program helped me be more attuned to creating and executing on the culture I envisioned for my company. I wanted our people to lead successful lives, both personally and professionally. I wanted them to come to work wanting to be here. And I wanted them to not only participate in our growth, but feel ownership in it." —*Dee M. Robinson, CEO, Robinson Hill, Inc.*

D0733391

"Getting clear on the culture of our community has given us powerful insights into who we represent and who we are here to serve. The whole process helped us to understand our strong cards and how to play them. Will Scott's process was not only helpful but was really enjoyable. The whole team was motivated by his approach and we came away with a stronger commitment and connection to our purpose and each other."
—*Maureen Muldoon, Founder SpeakEasy Spiritual Community.*

"In my 25 years helping leaders grow their companies, I've learned you can't retain and attract great talent without having a culture in place that is well-defined. The tools presented in *The Gift of Culture*—particularly the behavioral questions and CoreScore—allow leaders to do just that."
—*Todd Palmer, CEO Coach & Biz Therapist, Extraordinary Advisors.*

"Will Scott offered tremendous value to my business and team through his coaching services. His guidance around what he describes as 'culturally-conscious leadership', changed my approach to managing my business and team. With this new lens, I was able to lead my team in clarifying and defining our core purpose. This clarity not only energized my team but allowed us to better communicate how our work served our clients. With our core purpose defined and clearly communicated, we are able to connect with and retain our ideal clients more easily and effectively. Overall, his support has elevated our team culture as well as my own leadership and this book will be another valuable resource to further his great work."
—*Constantine Linos – Founder, CPL Investments.*

"We thoroughly enjoyed the exercises with Will. He is such a patient soul and really helped us dig deep to determine our Beliefs and to help us with the right imagery. I'm thrilled beyond words and have been sharing our experience with several people."—*President, Integrator, Partner, BCR Wealth Strategies & Founder, Female Integrator Mastermind.*

"Will has given our company what feels like an actual Gift of Culture and we will never be the same. This methodology of creating, owning, and living our values through every lens in the business has radically transformed our company." —*Matt Troyer, CEO, Emergent Group.*

"The moment you connect with or learn from Will you can tell he has lived this work in every area of his life. There's a joy, compassion and wisdom to the way he sees and talks about culture. He makes something that is usually hard to grasp and abstract relatable, accessible, and actionable through his book. Will Scott and his work on culture is delightful, inspiring and meaningful all around." —*Katie Greenman, Founder, HumanSide, Inc.*

"Will understands the importance of caring about how people feel in the workplace. And his easy-to-follow methods are a simple blueprint that every leader can use to make sure their team and company are performing."—*Rachel Nielson, CEO, Result Drivers.*

"Many of the leadership teams I work with are seeking ways to achieve Culture Fulfillment with meaningful, lasting results. Reading Will's first book, *The Culture Fix*, and becoming an Actuator with The Culture Fix Academy provided me with the tools I needed to help my clients achieve their Culture Fulfillment goals. Now, with *The Gift of Culture*, I have another tool in my toolkit to share with my clients, one that allows them to clearly understand the role of an Actuator and the role of the Culture Czar through the great storytelling of Everco's journey." —*Tim Sloane, CEO, The Sloane Agency.*

"I knew my company's culture was important, and Culture Fulfillment was exactly what I needed to define it and make it thrive."—*Mike Stratta, CEO, Arcalea.*

"Our investment in a formal culture program has created an atmosphere where culture has become the driving force toward our vision and related decision making. And we easily achieved a 10X return on our investment within the first 12 months of implementing Will's Culture Fulfillment ideas." —*Fred Pennell, CPA, CGMA, Managing Partner, Pennell CPA.*

The Gift of Culture

A Coach Transforms a Company's People and Profits by Applying 9 Deeds in 90 Days

by Will Scott

The Gift of Culture

A Coach Transforms a Company's People and Profits by Applying 9 Deeds in 90 Days

For general information about our products or services, please visit our website at **https://www.cultureczars.com/**, or contact the author at **will@cultureczars.com**.

Paperback: 978-1-7348853-4-7
Color Paperback: 978-1-7348853-6-1
Ebook: 978-1-7348853-5-4

Dedication

For every Culture Fulfillment project, we
receive as many gifts as we share.
This book is dedicated to our clients and to
the Actuator coaches who help them. From
them, we have learned as much as we have
taught.

Foreword

HAVING WORKED IN PREVIOUS environments where the culture didn't feel good, as CEO and COO of Tevera, we approached our existing core values with curiosity and caution. Though we did have an existing set of ideals, they didn't direct decisions and impact our every day.

From our own experience in leading, growing, and even selling other businesses, we understood that time and money are some of the most important resources. We wanted to use both wisely and decided that we wanted to go further than ever before in leading our new company with a culture-first mentality. After reading Will's *The Culture Fix*, we welcomed the wisdom that his experience provided and used it to help execute the vision we held. We started working together to take our already good culture and elevate it to be amazing. And tools like the CoreChart, CoreWorkflow, and CoreScore soon proved to be instrumental in how we led the company internally and how we communicated externally.

It wasn't as though we were starting from scratch. In fact, when we surveyed employees and asked how they might describe Tevera if it was a person, they responded with words like 'caring,' 'kind,' and 'honest.' It was heartening to hear these sentiments from our employees and even more validating to read similar responses from our customers in terms of the values they believed our employees displayed. Naturally we recognized the importance of integrating these values and spotted the inherent competitive advantage they represented.

Over the course of our Culture Fulfillment project, there were several visible signs that we were making a smooth and successful transition to having a valued culture. In fact, our surveys showed a 37.4 % improvement in approximately 4 months. Over time, our culture had become even stronger and increasingly storied, buoyed by our Notice & Nomination scheme.

While most stages were received with positivity and excitement, we certainly had a couple of minor stalls. For example, one afternoon, late in the process of finalizing our CoreVals, we received feedback from stakeholders about a revision. We called Will feeling defeated, because it felt like we were so close, yet so far from finalizing our CoreVals. Will's response was simple: "What a gift to have employees who care so much about making CoreVals more effective. Let's use this to do better, get more creative, and dig deeper until we land on something that excites them and hits the bullseye."

After weeks of discovery, design, and determination, we had our CoreVals and tools - like our CoreWorkflow - interlaced with values to use externally with customers and internally with sales and operations teams. These tools now influence everything from the website to social media and many places in between.

The result of our Culture Fulfillment process is nothing less than stunning, accomplishing far more than just words on paper. From the values to the CorePurpose on which they stand, the final result displays the entire story and spirit of our team. The CoreChart, which now lives on our website, has caused applicants to reach out and want to work for us because of the culture it conveys. Our CorePurpose statement not only motivates our team to know how close we are to fulfilling our vision, but also inspires their loyalty. The service-minded CorePurpose "we serve those who serve others so they can serve better" can be seen throughout our culture and the way we interact. Furthermore it has become our tagline and helps us connect with our customers and end users.

It is also gratifying to see strains of our story written in the pages of this book, *The Gift of Culture* and to see The Culture Fix Academy come to life, in part because we advised Will that the program could be taught to others and believed that propagating it to a wider audience more quickly would benefit businesses and employees everywhere.

Working on our culture was a gift we were happy to share with our owners, employees, and customers. In offering the gift to others, we continue to receive its benefits in return.

–Randy Zimmermann, CEO & Katie Sandquist, COO, Tevera

Acknowledgments

I would first like to acknowledge the people who will ultimately benefit from this book—employees everywhere who give of themselves every day to create, produce, serve, protect, deliver, and manage companies and organizations around the globe. Many of you are fortunate to work for organizations with great cultures where you can excel and contribute meaningfully to the world. You love where you work and why you work.

For others, however, you might not feel engaged at your workplace. I know from experience how challenging it is to dislike the working environment where you spend much of your time. My hope is that this book encourages you to champion a change in your organization that will transform it into a place you value.

I acknowledge all the leaders and C-suite executives who understand that culture creates loyal employees, efficient teams, and higher growth and profitability. To those leaders who have invested in culture and deliberately nurtured it, thank you for caring and for providing great environments for your teams.

To my clients, sawubona—I see you. I am grateful for your deliberation and for the value you place on creating culture champions. Your Churchillian efforts have yielded admirable cultures, tremendous growth, and greater profitability for the companies you lead. The abundancia that you demonstrate daily is reflected in your families, your teams, your colleagues, and your customers. You truly are leading a culture, not just a company. In particular, I'd like to thank Randy Zimmerman, Jeff Burton, Katie Sandquist, and Olivia Rodriguez of Tevera in Hudson, Wisconsin, who helped me bring this book to fruition because their project tracked perfectly with the writing of the book, and it was natural to adopt much of the actual project into our fable. Their Culture Fulfillment project was the baobab to this book. Other clients who inspired stories and images include: The Preferred Group, Conscious Connector, Pennell CPA, Next Day Dumpsters, Lextech, and SABRE.

Thanks to all the other business owners that I have been able to work with and who have contributed to this book and to my podcasts, many of them members of the Entrepreneurs Organization that has been so influential for my businesses and my personal growth.

Writing a book is a herculean effort and a deeply personal process. It would not have been possible without the help of my editor Summer Flynn, my book designer Joel Markquart, as well as the Culture Czars and The Culture Fix Academy teams.

Table of Contents

Introduction

I HAD THE FORTUNE of growing up in Zambia, surrounded by the natural rhythms of life. My playgrounds were the magnificent eucalyptus, mango, and stoic baobab trees where I created environments for myself and my friends. Whether it was a treehouse, a fort on stilts, a cave dwelling, or a sophisticated bamboo hut under a mango tree, there was one constant in each play structure: people to gather in them.

I quickly learned that anywhere people assembled, there was potential for drama, friction, and power struggles. It was important to me—having put the effort into creating these environments—that my friends be nice to each other and have positive experiences, so I drafted and posted rules to avoid negative interactions: No littering; Be nice; Keep this place secret; and—in the days before I learned the correct spelling and use of the phrase—No adults "aloud."

Looking back, I realized that posting treehouse rules ensured a safe space where everyone felt good and enjoyed being together. We were an exclusive group, bound by our agreed-upon guidelines. We knew what the boundaries were, how to interact, and ultimately, how each person could be a successful member of the whole. Our agreements created a common experience for us and guaranteed the most fun for the most people. The rules kept me—club president and peer—from having to constantly chastise my friends. Instead of grumbling about picking up trash, I could just point to the sign and say, "We all agreed not to litter." Done. Short conversation, no argument, everyone felt better. If friends were disrespecting each other, I could simply remind them,

"We agreed to be nice." I didn't have to reprimand, cajole, or teach during awkward moments of conflict. All I had to do was refer to a standard that we understood and to which we were committed.

With time, I learned that all effective organizations have rules—from companies large and small to the Navy Seals, to not-for-profits, and even national governments. These rules bind us together and provide a guideline for the benefit of future generations. After all, how would people in any country coexist without a shared constitution? These laws are nothing more than rules based on a set of values. We all know what they mean and what they stand for. Just as we couldn't harmoniously coexist without them, I don't know how any group operates without some code of conduct. Such documents serve the same purpose as my clubhouse rules once did—to provide a framework for how to live and work together. No matter the group's size or mission, people need boundaries to ensure they co-exist effectively, and they need a common language to navigate the inevitable ups and downs.

It's not enough to agree to unspoken rules; rather, we need codified guidelines. We need a language that empowers our ability to catch and correct behaviors in ways that don't demean others. This flattens a group's structure and allows each member to be empowered and invested. Of course, such codes only empower individuals when they've chosen to abide by them. Finding a group whose rules we accept and embrace allows us to feel welcomed, supported, and validated. It makes us feel at home.

Only later in my life did I fully understand the impression that my playful structures had on my life. In creating enticing places for friends to gather, I wasn't just building forts; I was learning my earliest lessons on how to build healthy communities and cultures. Those early experiences foretold my life's mission: To create environments where people thrive. Even at that formative age, I was defining my role as a future culture czar—a member who champions group culture and strives to exemplify its core values. Later in life, Simon Sinek helped me turn my mission into a purpose by completing the statement that drove my life: To create environments where people thrive so that they can be the best that they can be.

This mission stayed with me as I finished college and worked toward an MBA. With each job I held in the interim, I saw how a leader's values affected his/her workforce. I started thinking a lot about the environment of a work place—not just the physical space, but something intangible that manifested in tangible results: happy employees, less turnover, more efficient teams. I learned that the cultural environment made a direct impact on people's satisfaction, success and happiness.

I was already the founder of a SaaS supply chain software company in 2010, when I invested in a mobile app development company and took the roles of president and integrator. As a leader of one of the fastest-growing software companies in the country, I had the opportunity to cultivate the kind of culture our fictional company builds in this book. To this end, my leadership team and I created a workplace that was both fun and authentic. We took the time to intentionally discern the core values that would serve as our code of conduct. I wanted my team not only to be aware of our company's core values; I wanted to integrate them into our communal experience. I didn't want to tell the employees to feel something; I wanted to help them feel it. While core values marked the ideals by which we did business, living those ideals showed every member of the organization that we were in earnest. The team and I certainly took them seriously, and as a result, we grew 650 percent in just six years.

Due to the large investments made in culture, the company was driven by engaged and fulfilled teams. With time, other leaders and entrepreneurs took notice and asked me to replicate the program in their own organizations. As I spent more of my time consulting, I noted the practices and workflows that consistently worked with my clients—no matter the size or the industry. This proven process led to the publication of *The Culture Fix*® in 2020. Not long after, I recognized that the need for trained consultants was greater than the time I had available. The growing interest in culture and the need for trained implementers gave rise to The Culture Fix Academy™—the easiest fix for the hardest thing in business™ that allows members to join a supportive network and access a full suite of tools.

Helping corporate cultures transition to successful, united entities through the application of effective tools is about more than productivity and returns; it's about creating more successful companies with more fulfilled and dedicated workforces. I want people to be engaged in the workplace. I want people to feel good, to like where they work and who they work with.

Despite the large amount of time we spend at the workplace, Gallup research shows that only about 35 percent of employees are actually engaged in their work.[1] That means there is a 2:1 ratio of disengaged versus engaged people. What does it mean when an employee spends eight hours—a third

---

1   Jim Harter, "4 Factors Driving Record-High Employee Engagement in U.S.," Gallup.com (Gallup, February 4, 2020). http://www.gallup.com/workplace/284180/factors-driving-record-high-employment-engagement.aspx

of their day—actively disengaged? It means that though they may invest their time—because what choice do they have—they do not invest their passion or energy.

Engaged employees, on the other hand, are more loyal and more committed to workplace outcomes. They care about customers because they find meaning in their work and feel valued. They love where they work and who they work with and have a known purpose to their endeavors. As a result, they are more likely to be happy, loyal, and productive as well as to retain and attract clients.

Who is at fault for sweeping dissatisfaction? In the majority of instances, fault lies with leadership. Leaders control the environment and thus have the power to change the culture and create an environment where everyone thrives. Using a Culture Fulfillment model like the one put forth by The Culture Fix Academy and described in these pages, leaders can develop an environment where their employees are engaged, loyal, and fulfilled.

When people are only showing up for a paycheck, it's a travesty of leadership and a waste of talent. We want to change that—and our success with leaders and organizations proves that we can change that. One of the ways we measure company culture is by using an NPS® score to track employees' responses to the question: "What score would you give the company for having a great culture?" From my work with clients of all sizes and industries, it is not uncommon to achieve a 30 to 50 percent or more improvement in the NPS® score in just four months.

Leaders can make profound contributions to the world by creating environments where people thrive so they can be the best that they can be. When leaders, employees, customers, and vendors are aligned, the work feels easy. Rather than chasing some elusive work/life balance, people enjoy one fulfilling life because they are free to be themselves in the work environment, just as they are at home. Because work values are codified and lived, there is an alignment that allows all people to express themselves authentically and compassionately. The leaders model this by truly caring about how they make people feel. Their people, in turn, do the same. With time, the ripple effect of culture-conscious leadership extends beyond the walls of the workplace and into the lives, families, and communities of all the employees, customers, and vendors. Just imagine the global impact of this work!

In the past decade, we have seen many of the biggest companies thrive when their actions reflect dedication and commitment to their stated core values, and other companies floundered when their values were compromised in the pursuit of profits and a focus on shareholder value. In my experience, the most successful companies pay attention to stakeholder value, knowing that shareholder value will surely follow and be more robust in the long term. By considering stakeholders first and shareholder value second, the shift in the business will be evident from the inside out. Creating this passion and meaning for each and every stakeholder in an organization is imperative to success and generates a better culture for everyone involved. It also clearly communicates a purpose that explains the good the company does for the world.

The number of disengaged employees shows there is a global need for change. The time has never been more right for this kind of culture-conscious leadership. Through our work with organizations, and the work of The Culture Fix Academy Actuators, we want to promote a more conscious style of leadership that is values-based and driven by the good that the company does for people and planet. Many businesses have already begun the shift to this culture-conscious style of leadership wherein people care about their communities and the good they are doing, and it is showing in their success.

In the pages that follow, Culture Fulfillment—the same proven process I have been using for years—is shared in the form of a fable. Why a fable? Because this narrative art form emphasizes experience sharing, which is a much more powerful tool than telling or advising and allows for equal application of its lessons for all readers. We will meet a CEO who is making the transition from a traditional leadership style, focused on strategy and numbers, to a more culture-conscious one, focused on the way people feel and the commitment to their work.

As our leader learns, many organizations in crisis are there because of a failure of culture. If culture is not intentionally discerned and defined, then a default culture emerges that does not serve the organization. Equally ineffective or destructive is a defined culture that is not championed, not kept alive and thriving.

Culture Fulfillment is not about picking words from a list of values; it's about working closely with a trusted advisor—an Actuator who moves the team to action—to uncover what is unique about the people, the culture, and the purpose. Though it is possible to cultivate a valued culture internally, there is a profound benefit from bringing in an outside coach who can make objective observations and offer varied experiences. This is especially helpful when companies want to quickly address their culture or secure it before exponential growth. One additional benefit—as our leader learns in the following chapters—is that having an Actuator allows her to sit at the table with her team rather than facilitate. She's not above them, but rather among them.

Using practical, step-by-step tools, I hope this book ignites the entrepreneurial business community with the desire and the confidence to cultivate great cultures in their own organizations. Though the organization presented here is fictional, the issues and conflicts are real experiences that many of my clients have faced.

This book is for anyone who wants to live a holistic, healthy life across all spheres—work, home, play, travel, and beyond:

- It's for leaders who want engaged employees, increased productivity, higher workforce retention, and empowered teams;
- It's for managers who think the way people act and feel is more important than policies and procedures;
- It's for employees who are working in dysfunctional cultures and are seeking ways to influence their company's leaders and teammates;
- And it's for consultants, coaches, and Actuators who share a passion for connecting with organizations in deep and meaningful ways.

What is there to lose from running a culture-first organization? Nothing! In fact, it's a great way to have meaningful fun with your team. You may be a hard-driving CEO who cares about results, but it's okay to have some fun and feel good about it. Not only is it okay; your team will love you for it, stay with you longer, and give you more, ultimately driving your business to reach its full potential.

Despite the measurable returns on culture, many leaders don't necessarily know how to create a great culture. As we will explore in these pages, the work involves more than having an outsider stamp a prescriptive formula of culture on an organization. It's about fulfilling the best of what already exists within. In reality, it's much easier to have a great culture with twenty-five employees; it's much harder with 250 or more employees. Regardless, if the challenge isn't met, people don't feel safe, empowered, or engaged.

From the time I was a child in Zambia building clubhouses for my friends, my major impetus has been inclusion. I have always had the desire and the need to include people. Ultimately, this is what a corporate culture can do for a workplace. It's not just about making the work environment more enriching; it's also about making each and every individual who you lead feel like they belong to something bigger than themselves. It's for this reason that we call culture a "gift." Not only does The Gift of Culture show what a great culture can look like, it also offers the steps it takes to achieve it, and the tools it takes to sustain it.

To reverse the ratio of employee disengagement, leaders need to lead with culture. No other initiative brings greater rewards for all members of a team than Culture Fulfillment. Any smart business makes investments in its greatest assets, so if leaders believe people are the greatest asset, provide them with the greatest environment. After all, investing in culture is investing in people, and the good news is that it's never too late to lead your organization towards a values-based culture.

Whenever I built a clubhouse like this one in Zambia, I would post rules, not unlike core values in companies today.

Chapter 1: The Call

WITH HER HAND POISED on the front door of Everco Marketing, Leslie froze. She felt the familiar tightness in her chest as she prepared to open the door and face what was inside—people and interactions that drained her. Some might call this the Monday blues, but she understood it was more than that. Last Friday had been one of the most challenging days of her career. It felt like a bad dream, but as she opened the door to her company and walked inside to see the darkened corner office, she understood it was a reality: Oliver—her Chief Operations Officer, and her oldest and most trusted partner—had left. His absence would be difficult enough, but learning that he was leaving to join the team of their biggest client, Whale Services, was a major blow, personally and professionally. Now she had no COO and had lost her biggest client. In one short day, her confidence had taken as big a hit as her revenue.

Despite the dread she felt, she knew the work wouldn't wait. She took a breath and walked inside the building.

There had been some earlier signs that Oliver was dissatisfied, though she hadn't recognized them. How many times had Oliver expressed frustrations about how the team communicated with each other? Often, she realized, and with more frequency in the last couple of years.

"There's no accountability!" he'd complain. "No one does what they say they are going to do."

She remembered he'd requested a code of conduct. Had she taken any steps to create one? She knew they had created core values—though she couldn't remember them at the moment—but what more did he expect her to do? She had been swamped in the last few years as the company had grown quickly, filling new positions and juggling more clients. She knew Oliver had issues with some of their people, but she didn't dare let any of the original team go. She needed them, and she thought that if she let them go, Everco would flounder. Surely the teammates' loyalty to Everco over the years should count for something.

When Leslie had started Everco Marketing five years ago, she had been full of energy and enthusiasm. She'd loved being an entrepreneur surrounded by people who shared her passions. Some of her earliest business lessons had come from watching her mother work tirelessly all her life. When Leslie had interned for her mother's not-for-profit, she'd seen how the organization had excelled in their services but struggled with their marketing. They had done great work, but not enough people knew they existed, or were aware of the good that they did in the world. Leslie understood early on that a charitable organization is only as healthy as its flow of donors. After college, Leslie had worked at a marketing firm that focused solely on for-profits. Though it lacked the same purpose and drive of her mother's organization, she'd observed how the firm leveraged branding and knew the same strategy could benefit non-profits.

Fueled by her passion for creativity and marketing, she'd started Everco to help charitable organizations get their messages out to wider audiences so they might have the revenues they needed to fulfill their missions.

In those early days, she'd spent her time surrounded by people who were as passionate as she was. She used to be excited to come to work every day. Her clients inspired her, and her people motivated her to be the best leader she could be. She wanted the workplace to be playful, so she invested in a ping-pong table. She remembered the day it had arrived at the office. They had just landed the Whale Services account, and she knew they would be working long hours to deliver their services to the biggest client they had signed. When the table had arrived, her employees cheered and challenged each other to what would become a heated tournament series. This was also around the time they started "Beer O'Clock" at 4 pm on Fridays. She was hoping this would create opportunities for teammates to connect, get to know each other, and celebrate the week's work.

But now, things were different. As she walked the hall to her office, she remembered asking Oliver if he was leaving because of money.

"It's not the money," he'd said. He had looked as miserable as she'd felt.

"Then what is it?" she'd pleaded.

"It's everything. It's the feeling here. The apathy. It's the way we talk to each other and... actually, the way we don't talk to each other."

Though Leslie still thought his judgments were harsh, it had tuned her into something she felt, too. Was there indeed something dysfunctional about Everco's work environment? As the CEO, Leslie believed her role was to handle strategies. She focused on facts, not feelings.

She set her things down on her desk, ignored her inbox, and headed straight to Hilda's office.

Hilda was relatively new in her role as their Human Resources Director. If anyone could fix Everco's "dysfunction" in the workplace, surely it was her. Leslie entered without knocking and startled Hilda from the email she was reading.

"Do you think we have a bad work environment?" Leslie blurted.

"Well, hi, Leslie. That's quite a heavy question first thing on a Monday morning," Hilda laughed.

"I'm serious. Oliver left because he didn't like the way it felt here. Do you agree with that?"

Hilda was silent for a moment as if searching for the right words. "I think there are some great things about working here. I also think there are opportunities for improvement."

"Like what?" Leslie prodded.

"Well, I think there are ways we could work better as a team. And make everyone feel…more supported, more valued… and connected."

"Do you think that's why Oliver left?"

"In my opinion, that is why people leave, yes."

Leslie knew that Hilda had a lot of experience. When she and Oliver first interviewed her, they had been struck by her enthusiasm and strategic thinking. She'd seemed like she genuinely wanted to work here. Even so, Leslie was shocked that Hilda had left her previous job of ten years to work for Everco.

"Did you like your previous job?"

Hilda's face spread into a slow smile. "I did. I loved it. In fact, some of my co-workers are still my closest friends."

"Then why did you leave? Why did you come here?"

"I came here to advance my career. I went from assistant HR there to Director here. I recognized an opportunity to run an HR department the way I wanted to and to create something special. And with how quickly Everco was growing, I was excited to be a part of that. It seemed fun. Like those videos of Fred singing karaoke at the family picnics."

Leslie laughed with Hilda. She had forgotten about the picnics. Those were fun. They hadn't had one in a couple of years, though she couldn't recall why. She stood to leave and then turned back.

"Do you think people are happy here?" she asked.

Hilda laughed. "I don't know. Do you feel happy here?"

Leslie wasn't sure if this was a rhetorical question or not. She chose not to respond.

Leaving Hilda's office, she felt the urge to talk to her Leadership Team—or at least what was left of it. She headed toward Richard's office, but as usual, it was dark. Richard was their Chief Revenue Officer, and his philosophy was that if he was in the office, then he wasn't doing his job. Richard lived for sales. It was all he cared about. Over the years, he had upset many of her employees because of his abrasiveness, but that was just his personality. He was a jokester and a cad. Truthfully, Leslie overlooked these qualities because of his ability to bring in sales. They couldn't have survived the last five years without him.

She passed Richard's door and knocked on the window of Fred's office—her Chief Financial Officer. He was on the phone but motioned for her to come in and take a seat. She could tell from the conversation that he was talking to his wife. They had been married for many years, and the team often joked they couldn't go an hour without speaking. Their conversations were usually about daily logistics. Today it sounded like she had some errands for him to run after work. He gruffly told her he'd call her back.

"Another day, another to-do list," he complained.

Leslie grimaced. She knew Fred had a softer side, but he'd showed it less and less often over the years. She had known Fred since childhood, and though he'd never been famous for his personality, he was one of her mother's trusted advisors. Fred had been her first hire and had been loyal to Everco since the beginning. These days, that was all she needed.

"Hey, Fred. How was your weekend?"

"I spent it running numbers, and I have to tell you, without Whale Services, we're in a bind."

"Did you come up with any solutions?"

"Yes. Fire that deadbeat Richard who never can find the time to grace us with his presence."

"Well, that's why I came to talk to you. Not to fire Richard, of course, but to ask you how you like working here?"

He laughed. "I've been here five years, and now you ask?"

"Yes, I'm asking. Would you say that it feels good to work here?"

Now he grew serious. "We're not here to feel things, Leslie. We're here to work. Now if you have a problem with something I'm doing, you just come out and say it."

"No, no. You're fine, Fred. I was just wondering. I'll let you get back to work."

He grumbled something about not having work to do if they couldn't replace their lost client.

She left his office, feeling deflated.

Headed back to her own office, Leslie remembered that for Everco's first two years, she had maintained a healthy work/life balance. She woke early to spend time with her son before heading to work, full of enthusiasm. Though she worked long days, she came home feeling energized by what she had contributed to her teams and clients and brought that home to her family and friends in the form of joy and inspiration. On weekends, they went for long hikes or bike rides. She was proud that her son saw the work she did, but she also wanted him to see her take time for herself and her loved ones.

Over time, however, as the business grew, her home life became more harried and frantic. More employees didn't mean more helpers; it meant more people needed help. And the newer hires were not as reliable as her original team had been. There never seemed to be enough time for her family, her friends, her health. When she was at home, she stressed about work; when she was at work, she worried about home. Now, without Oliver, her work life was sure to become even more complicated.

Settling into her office chair, she understood her trajectory if she didn't do something: she would lose people she valued. Something had to change. Oliver's leaving was an opportunity to wake up to the importance of how it felt to work here. As the leader of Everco, she was uniquely positioned to revive the joy and enthusiasm. But how? And when was she going to find the time to do it? She had already been stretched too thin even before Oliver left.

She knew leadership was hard, but she didn't realize it was so lonely.

Leadership doesn't have to be lonely.

She remembered someone saying that at last month's networking event—during a presentation about values. She'd had a conversation with the speaker after. She didn't recall the details, but she remembered how present he had seemed, contrasted with the hurried business leaders around them. He'd asked her a lot of questions about Everco. Hadn't he given her a book?

She scanned her shelves and found it—*The Culture Fix.* She opened to the handwritten note: "Strategy is to thought as culture is to feelings. Andy" Yes, Andy. That was what they'd talked about: the importance of culture in the workplace. She wished now that she had paid more attention when he spoke.

She flipped through the book and landed on a passage: "You may think you're dedicated, but if you are not living, breathing, and talking about those values—keeping them alive—then the culture doesn't thrive and your organization's performance doesn't drive to its full potential."

She looked up at the small core values poster hanging on her wall—*Integrity, Respect, Teamwork, Quality, Honesty.* That described the workplace Oliver was seeking. But how could she make the words on the wall become the behavior in the workplace? She considered the ping-pong table, the COO's office, the core values—all empty. She was suddenly aware that ping-pong and beer carts do not make a great culture. So what does make a great culture?

How did she miss the signs that the culture wasn't thriving? How had she gotten so wrapped up in leading a team that she forgot about leading *people*—people with passions, families, commitments, goals, feelings? She remembered from her early work experience that if individuals felt committed, then they were more loyal and attracted more like them. Teams needed to like working together, and they needed to know they were doing something meaningful for the world. Maybe then they would also enjoy ping-pong, beer, and family picnics. But maybe the culture came first?

If she could create an environment that reflected any of the sentiments on her wall poster, then the culture wouldn't chase her best people away. She knew that even if there was a large market for her services, she needed great teams organized in a great environment to make it successful.

She grabbed her phone and dialed the number Andy had written under his name. When he answered, she reintroduced herself.

"Leslie! I'm so glad you reached out. How are you? And how are things at Everco?"

Leslie decided it was best to get right to it. "Not good, Andy. We've got some issues." She told him all about Oliver's leaving and the blow it landed to her revenues and Leadership Team. She longed for a great company and for people who liked each other, and were as committed as she was. Or as she used to be. She wanted them to get along, but a few dysfunctional relationships had created a tough dynamic. She also shared how she personally felt and the toll that the situation was taking.

"But that's not all," she continued. "There are other issues."

Andy welcomed her to share, and Leslie found that once she started, she couldn't stop.

"I can't hire good people or keep good people. People don't share openly. We're always behind, and the quality of our services has decreased. Our clients aren't happy. We're treading water. I'm treading water. Can you help?"

"I hear you, Leslie, and I want to help. Tell me, how would you describe your culture at Everco?"

Leslie talked about the low commitment of her teams. She said everyone was watching the clock, and some were out the door by five o'clock each day. She also told him that people didn't do what they said they would and that she didn't know how to correct it.

"Do you have a cultural definition describing your core values, attributes, or beliefs?" Andy asked.

"We've got some rote words that we don't have any attachment to. In fact, I can only remember them by looking at the poster," Leslie admitted.

"Tell me how you are doing. What's going on with you personally as a leader?"

Leslie had never been asked this before, but she answered honestly. "I'm stressed. I thought once I got to this point, I'd be able to relax, to really enjoy life. But I'm not. I don't. I didn't feel this way when my company only had ten employees."

When she was finished, Andy explained that culture was the hardest thing in business. "Luckily, I have a solution. I'm an Actuator for a Culture Fulfillment program, the same one described in the book that I gave you. It's not your typical consulting program where we stamp a program on your business. As Actuators, we want to understand the DNA of your organization, and then we bring our energy and help move you to fulfill the best of what exists. If you and your Leadership Team can give me about an hour of your time, I can offer you the Gift of Culture meeting. I guarantee you will get a lot of value from the meeting, but there's no obligation."

They settled on the meeting details, and when Leslie hung up, she let out a sigh. It felt like a breath she had held for hours, days, even months. She felt a small glimmer of hope.

Chapter 2: The Gift of Culture

LESLIE THREW THE OFFICE door open with her one free finger and almost dropped her phone. She had been trying to connect with this potential client all week and had finally reached his assistant. Now she waited on hold. She spied Andy looking intently at the art on the reception walls. As she walked in, he turned to her and smiled. She nodded, held up a finger as if to say "Hold on," and rushed to her office. While classical music played in her ear, she unloaded her arms and took a breath. She was nervous about today. She didn't know why. Maybe because choosing to invest in Everco's culture was the first decision she had made without Oliver by her side. Or maybe because she was scared to learn how bad their culture problem really was.

"Hello, Leslie. Are you there?"

Leslie startled and fumbled with the phone. "Oh, yes, hi, Walter. Hi." Leslie regained her composure and made obligatory small talk before cutting to the chase. "Walter, you've been dragging your feet for weeks. What's it going to take to close this deal?"

The line was silent.

"Walter? Walter, are you there?" She heard pieces of his garbled reply. "Walter, I can't hear you." Leslie walked outside to the hall. "Is this better, Walter? Can you hear me?"

No reply.

Leslie ran to reception and repeated, "Are you still there, Walter?"

Andy looked up to her with a hopeful grin, and she pointed to the phone.

"I'm on the phone, and I really need to take this. Go on down to the conference room. I'll be right in." She turned her attention back to the phone. "Walter? Walter? Can you hear me?"

Leslie found a spot in the common room where the reception was clearer. Walter was talking about the challenges of his company's campaign. She couldn't believe she was going to lose this project. She and Walter had a long-standing business friendship, which was how she could tell he had chosen another firm.

"Look, Walter, I have a meeting to get to. Is Everco in or out?"

"I'm sorry, Leslie. I just can't go forward with Everco."

"Can I ask why, Walter? Were we underbid?"

"No, no, Leslie. It's not that. It's just that...well, to be frank, I don't get a good vibe from Richard. I think my team would prefer to align with another firm."

"Walter, I hear what you're saying, but you wouldn't be working with Richard. You'd be working with our creative team. Richard just helps seal the deal."

"Well, he didn't seal this deal. In fact, he put off some of my team, and I wouldn't be doing my job if I didn't respect and protect my people. It's just that...your teams don't seem to care as much as they used to. I'm sorry, Leslie."

Leslie felt like someone had punched the air out of her. She thanked him for his time and for being honest, and wished him good luck on the project. She took a breath and headed back to the conference room.

***

"It's Oliver's fault that we have to sit through this meeting. If he hadn't left and gotten Leslie all rattled, I'd be finishing my coffee in peace." Fred settled into his well-worn seat at the conference table.

Hilda finished preparing her tea and took a seat across from Fred. "Actually, I'm excited. I started reading the book Leslie had, and I think there might be something useful in this for us."

"Useful? It's just another meeting," Fred retorted.

Andy stepped into the room. "Good morning. Am I in the right place?"

As Hilda introduced herself and got him some water, Andy set up his computer and asked Fred how long he had worked at Everco.

"Long enough to resent it," Fred shot back.

Andy was definitely in the right place.

Leslie walked in and thanked him for coming. She asked if they could dive right in.

Andy sensed that she was rushed, tense. "Is this everyone on the Leadership Team?"

"All the good ones," Fred muttered.

Leslie interjected, "We're missing Richard, our CRO. I thought he was joining us virtually, but maybe not. We can catch him up later."

Andy had always been good at reading people in his emotionally intelligent way. This team was no different. He'd felt the tension as soon as he'd walked in the door. People seemed stressed and dismissive of one another. This might have made some coaches nervous, but not Andy. He was confident he could help this team and felt energized by the opportunity.

"Great! Then let's get started."

Andy sensed that the entire room felt rushed, not just Leslie. Although he appreciated the time they were devoting to him and hearing about Culture Fulfillment, he wanted to slow the pace. He began by asking them how open they were to the meeting and to talking about culture. The responses were curt, and he sensed they were thinking about the work that awaited them.

"I have found that setting a pace for the meeting helps us all be present and makes the meeting more valuable. I invite you all to take a few slow breaths with me." After a few moments, he continued. "Ok, let's get started. Before we move on to talk about the program, let's take a quick poll: What score would you give Everco for having a great culture? Choose one to ten with ten being the best. Hilda, let's start with you."

Hilda looked surprised and thought for a few seconds. "Six," she answered.

"Ok, what would you say, Fred."

"If I have to pick a number? Four," he said immediately, without looking up from the pile of papers he often carried.

Andy looked to Leslie. She didn't know how to answer. "Five? Six?" she answered.

"Okay, that's helpful to know," Andy continued. "This is actually why *The Culture Fix* started—for companies like yours. Its mission is to usher in a decade of conscious leadership, making sure employees feel fulfilled, loyal and engaged, no longer working to live but rather having one fulfilling life. I started my career as an independent coach, focusing on business operations. Over time, though, I noticed that many of my clients shared the same misalignment between leadership teams, cultures, and behaviors. I came across *The Culture Fix*, and as I read it, I appreciated that the book was practical, not just theoretical. I reached out to the author to learn more. And then I followed my head and my heart to become an Actuator so that I can help move teams to fulfill the culture they've always wanted. That's why I'm excited to be here with you today, sharing the Culture Fulfillment program so that your teams can love where they work and why they work."

Andy asked about the history of Everco and made note of the team's responses. Most of the questions were easy to answer until he inquired, "What's been the worst moment in Everco's history?"

Fred looked up from his stack of papers and told Andy about losing clients during the recession some years earlier.

That was indeed a bad time, but if Leslie answered honestly, she would tell Andy that the worst moment was last week when she lost her biggest client on the same day she lost her COO.

When Andy asked about their growth goals, Fred rattled off their revenue targets and Hilda talked about increasing their employee numbers.

Leslie wondered what her own goals were. She desired more time. She needed more people. She wished for teams who delivered on time and collaborated well. She wanted less waste and more communication. What would it take to get Everco to be all that she wanted it to be?

Her reverie was broken when Andy asked, "How would you describe your culture today?"

Leslie answered, "Well we appreciate success and growth, but some good people leave. And the doors spin at five o'clock. What does that say? Also, we don't really know if remote work is successful or not."

Hilda added, "People aren't open here. They're guarded, not themselves."

Fred joined in. "No one follows the processes. I can't even get invoices submitted on time."

Andy listened intently and responded, "All of these are symptoms of cultural issues. The good news here is that these can all be addressed by investing in culture. Can you give me some values that are present at Everco?"

After several moments of silence, Hilda spoke up. "I'm not sure, but it feels like pressure because we're making the same mistakes repeatedly. It makes each day stressful."

Andy recognized what was happening. The culture needed a fix, but no one wanted to share just how bad things were. He knew he would learn more about the current culture if Everco moved ahead and allowed him to do his surveys and interviews with leaders and employees. For now, he would move on and tell them more about how he could help.

'The purpose of Culture Fulfillment is to help a company bring its culture alive, make it thrive, and use it to drive performance so that employees are engaged and feel their work has meaning." Next, Andy shared some startling research

Client Profile

Company: Everco

Leadership Team:

· Leslie L., CEO

· Hilda H., HR

· Fred F., CFO

· Richard R., CRO (not present)

Culture Liaison: TBD

How many years have you been in business? 5

How many total employees do you have including remote and on-site? 75

How many employees do you think you will add in several years? 25+

How many locations do you have? 1 physical plus remote and WFH

Give a brief history of your company from when you started to present day:

Everco is a marketing company, specializing in non-profit work. They have experienced fast growth in the last several years and expect that to continue.

What's been the best moment in your company's history?

Their largest client, Whale Charities, raised a record number of funds as a result of a campaign that was designed and executed by Everco.

What's been the worst moment in the company's history?

During the recession almost three years earlier, Everco lost half its clients because when corporate profits decreased, so did donations.

What are the growth goals over next 2 years?

· Get to 100 employees
· 10 more clients
· Grow by another $3 million

What are your revenues now? $7 million

What are your anticipated revenues in 2 years? $10 million

How would you describe your culture today?

Stressful, lots of pressure, making the same mistakes repeatedly. But good people who care.

In a few words, what would you like the culture to feel like in the future?

Less stressful, better teamwork, feel like we care about each other, and can trust each other to do what we say we're going to do. More balance and motivation.

showing that the percentage of "not-engaged" and "actively disengaged" employees hit 65 percent in the global workforce. "This is nothing less than a malaise, a real illness that is affecting workplaces around the world. We're on a mission to cure this."

Leslie's shoulders relaxed as Andy spoke. He was describing exactly what she knew Everco needed. But could she get her team to agree? She looked at Fred, who was tugging on his beard and reading the papers in front of him. He was clearly not invested in this meeting. Hilda, on the other hand, took notes and nodded enthusiastically as Andy spoke about how having purpose fulfilled the human need to feel connected and valued.

"We believe employees can love where they work, who they work with, and feel like they are doing something meaningful for the world," Andy explained.

Next, he displayed what he called a CoreChart—an infographic that combined a company's core values and CorePurpose. He explained how The Culture Fix Academy had four CoreVals: Churchillian, Baobab, Sawubona, and Abundancia. Leslie immediately noticed how unique those values were. She especially resonated with Sawubona, which Andy shared was a Zulu greeting meaning "I see you" but went further to imply the recognition of worth and dignity in each person. He said this was a value that showed human connection, care, and inclusivity. The values before her were not the tired, vague generalities Everco had chosen. Seeing the values graphically excited her. *This is what Everco needs and what I need*, she thought.

As Andy explained each value, she saw how having the values written down and paired with a unique illustration made them seem more memorable, more unique. Andy brought the message home with what he called a CoreVals Address and in a few minutes conveyed a descriptive feeling of the organization that was memorable, palpable, and seemed ustainable—frankly, an organization that one would wish to be associated with.

TCF Academy CoreChart

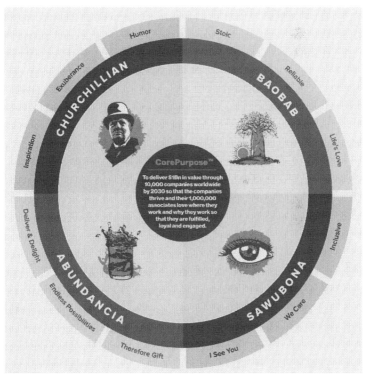

Andy shared that another reason to lead with a culture-first mentality was to avoid catastrophic scandals like the ones happening every week in the news.

o many companies write glowing core values, only to all over them in practice. It's pervasive among public companies to write what they think they should write and then pay no attention to them. If more CEOs led according to the values of the company, there would be a lot fewer issues in business, fewer scandals to recover from, and fewer people—including customers, employees and shareholders—getting hurt. If we lead with stakeholder value, shareholder value will surely follow, but too often core values are ignored in favor of a short-term focus on shareholder value and profits. This is a very dangerous practice which will eventually come undone."

Then Andy shared a list of common culture problems he had helped teams with in the past.

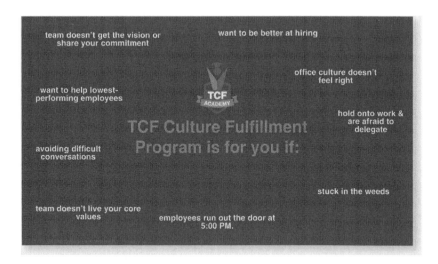

"Do any of these look familiar?" Andy asked with a smile. All heads—even Fred's—nodded.

"Well, all these ailments are addressed by culture, and we believe the easiest fix for the hardest thing in business is Culture Fulfillment. And why do we consider culture a gift? Because culture-first companies transform people and their work environments for the better. Without a methodology, however, the transformation is elusive. *The Culture Fix* framework and tools provide a proven roadmap for transforming your culture. I will leave you with copies of *The Culture Fix*." Andy reached into his bag and put some books on the table. "Even if you don't move forward with Everco's Culture Fulfillment, the book and what we share today will offer you practical steps to enhance the best of what already exists within your organization. If you do move forward with Culture Fulfillment, the culture boost will be a real gift to all the stakeholders involved with the company. You will also experience a better work environment as well as have the tools and a common language to sustain it."

Andy explained that the process of Culture Fulfillment was not like the typical consulting experience. Rather than stamp a prescribed system on Everco, he would spend time with the organization over the next four months and through monthly workshops, weekly coaching calls, surveys, and interviews, arrive at a clear cultural definition of the best of what already existed within Everco.

"As an Actuator, it is my job, in partnership with a Culture Liaison at Everco, to move your teams to action, to model how to talk, listen, and affirm, so that we can transform how people behave and interact. Let me show you how it works."

Andy introduced the 9 Deeds Model and detailed the three phases they would work through with their teams to improve their culture.

"The first phase of TCF Fulfillment focuses on how to bring core values alive," he explained. "During the initial

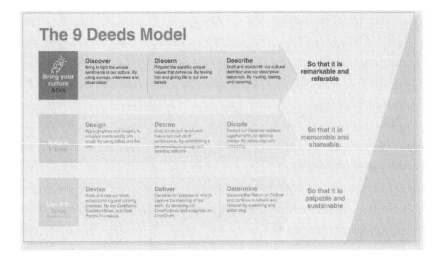

Discover phase, we will use surveys, interviews, and observations to unearth the unique sentiments of our culture. We will also Discern to pinpoint the specific, unique values that define us by feeling into—and giving life to—our core beliefs. Next, we will muse, test, and hone to Describe our CoreVals with descriptive behaviors or subtexts. At the end of Phase I: Alive, we will find ourselves with a memorable, engaging, and effective set of values that are remarkable and referable with executives, employees, and corporate partners all moving in flow with these values, Everco's workplace will be on its way to becoming a place where the culture is Alive."

"In Phase II: Thrive," he continued on, "we memorialize your core values visually to help employees and partners remember them. A common misconception is that core values are for internal consumption only—that they will never be communicated outside the organization. That's a big mistake and a missed opportunity."

Leslie repositioned in her seat. She thought back to the bland poster on her wall listing their core values. She was

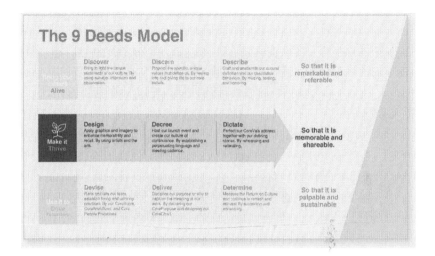

suddenly embarrassed by how little time and energy she had invested in drafting them.

"You're leading a culture that extends beyond the four walls of the company," Andy reminded them. "Core values can be effective when floated downstream to clients and the general public, and upstream to vendors and colleagues. It helps spread your unique culture to the greater community, aligning your best clients and vendors with your company's mission. First, we will focus on the Design of your core values. Applying graphics and imagery enhances memorability and recall. Next, we focus on Decree. Here, we host a launch event and create continuity of messaging by establishing a perpetuating language and meeting cadence. Finally, we will Dictate your CoreVals address—using the defining stories from Phase 1. Essentially, in this phase, we take the values off the wall and—by making them memorable and shareable— plant them in the hearts and minds of your people—and beyond! At the end of Phase II: Thrive, you will have visually appealing core values that are memorable."

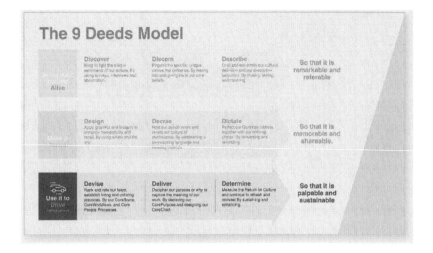

"With this work behind you," Andy went on, "you will be ready to move on to Phase III: Drive. Our first deed of this phase is to Devise practices and strategies to harness your Core Values that will ultimately drive your organization's performance to new heights. We will rank and rate your team and applicants using the CoreScore, and establish hiring and unhiring practices. This is also where we teach how to use Notice & Nominate and Catch & Correct. The next stage is a profound moment for your organization when you Deliver your organization's purpose or why to capture the meaning of your team's work. This is shared through your declaration of your CorePurpose and CoreChart. Finally, in the Determine phase, we measure the Return on Culture and continue to refresh and reinvest so that your culture is palpable and sustainable."

Andy's voice grew even more enthusiastic as he talked about the results. "After working through the three phases of Culture Fulfillment, you can expect changes from your new culture-first mindset. Not only will you see the changes in the contentment of your workforce, you will also find that you are leading a more competent and united team, thus making your own schedule and workload more streamlined and efficient."

Leslie's mind stuck on his words streamlined, efficient. She thought of the ripple effects that Culture Fulfillment could have on her personally. As if he could read her thoughts, Andy continued to talk more about the benefits to the Leadership Team.

"As leaders of a culture-first team, you'll be able to give tough conversations finite boundaries and clear-cut resolutions; educate and empower employees to make decisions in line with values, rather than having to delegate or authorize individual actions; free up your time for executive duties by relying on qualified staff members; be more accurate and successful at hiring for cultural fit; and give your clients something to believe in. After implementing Culture Fulfillment, you'll soon find that Everco's value culture has come alive in the minds and lives of your employees, allowing them to thrive in their roles and drive the performance of your company. The costs required to realize this vision come at a minimum compared to the growth you could see, both on the bottom line of your business and in the hearts of your people."

Leslie was ready to try it, but she knew her team would be hesitant, especially Fred. In an effort to get ahead of his skepticism, she raised her hand.

"What if some of the team is…hesitant?" Leslie asked.

"That's a great question, Leslie. I would suggest that you lead with outcomes. First of all, we can measure culture. One of the ways we do this is by testing the NPS® score of the employees in answer to the question: 'What score would you give the company for having a great culture?' It's not uncommon to achieve significant improvements in the score in just four months with Culture Fulfillment from TCF Academy. In addition, here is a list of other benefits you will enjoy."

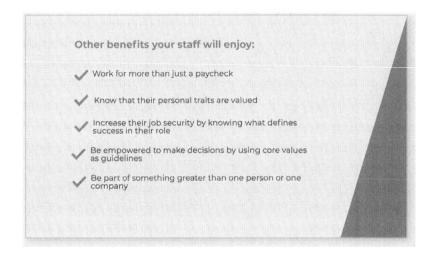

Other benefits your staff will enjoy:

✓ Work for more than just a paycheck

✓ Know that their personal traits are valued

✓ Increase their job security by knowing what defines success in their role

✓ Be empowered to make decisions by using core values as guidelines

✓ Be part of something greater than one person or one company

Leslie hoped that Fred was paying attention, but since he still stared at the papers in front of him, it was hard to tell. "We're definitely interested," Leslie replied. "And you're describing some of the exact issues we want to remedy. What can we expect in terms of time and resources?"

"Let me answer that using the Culture Fulfillment Model. The next step in the process is a forty-five-minute virtual Kickoff Call using a tool such as Zoom. During this call, we will discuss your team's initial thoughts about culture. We will also decide on a Culture Team, composed of your Leadership Team and any designated culture czars. Those are team members who exemplify Everco's core values and are champions of culture. During the Kickoff call, I will also explain how to administer a series of unique surveys to better understand how your leaders, teams, and clients view your existing culture."

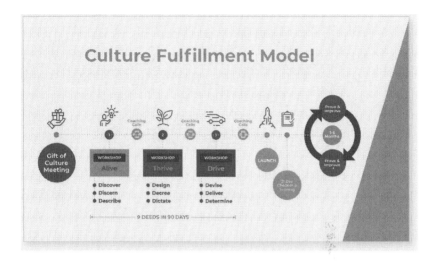

As Andy explained what they would cover in each workshop, Leslie wondered what he might uncover during the surveys and interviews, and the familiar tension returned to her shoulders. She knew this might be uncomfortable at first, but if it worked, it would be worth it.

Andy told them that all three workshops culminated in the Launch Event—the unveiling of the organization's graphics. Leaders and Culture Czars would present the cultural definitions and accompanying stories. "When we complete the Launch Event, you will all have a clear strategy for integrating the core values into hiring and unhiring practices and nomination awards, as well as events and meetings."

Hilda was smiling now. Andy was describing the exact thing she knew Everco needed, and some of the things she had wanted to implement but hadn't known how. With their recent growth, she had hired without any clear strategy. Though some of the new hires were quite strong, others didn't seem invested in Everco or the work they did.

Andy told them he would return several weeks after the Launch Event for a Check-in and Training. "Using surveys and interviews, we will determine how 'real' your values feel to team members and leaders. In this training, we will discuss how to continue infusing core values into the day-to-day culture. We recommend pulsing this every three- to six-months with our Prove & Improve cycle."

Leslie wondered how she would keep the momentum going on this project, but then Andy explained that in the weeks between events, he would hold coaching calls with an appointed Culture Liaison to keep things moving and to coordinate the activities between the scheduled events. Leslie's shoulders relaxed when she realized she wouldn't be leading this initiative.

"And that is TCF's Culture Fulfillment Program. Using the 9 Deeds of Alive, Thrive, and Drive, your core values will come alive, make your people and processes thrive, and drive your organization toward its full potential." Andy displayed one last slide. "Here is a list of the types of results you can expect from investing in your culture."

At Completion:

✓ Everyone is accountable, on the same page, and pulling together

✓ Teams make decisions the same way that leadership would

✓ Difficult conversations that promote healthy, safe relationships are embraced, not avoided

✓ The right people are hired and retained and the cultural misfits are respectfully unhired

✓ Measurable and significant increases in sales and profits are credited to the culture

As Andy read the list aloud, Leslie realized she had been running Everco on strategies and numbers but ignoring culture. She focused on ping-pong tables and beer carts and thought that was enough. She'd never realized she could use values to rank and rate her current and future employees. Even though she knew that the gift Andy offered was the exact one Everco needed, she knew some of her leaders— mainly Fred and Richard—would need some convincing. She thanked Andy for his time and told him the team needed a day to think about it. Fred immediately grabbed his stack of papers and left the room.

Andy told Leslie and Hilda to take the time they needed and agreed it was important that the entire Leadership Team was on board.

As Hilda thanked Andy and helped him gather his belongings, Leslie muttered, "That might be the hardest part."

Chapter 3: Kickoff

AT THE NEXT DAY'S LEADERSHIP Team meeting, Leslie asked Hilda whether or not she wanted to proceed with Culture Fulfillment. If Hilda was honest, she would have told Leslie she was nervous. Not because she didn't think Everco would benefit, but because she wondered if she might not benefit. As HR Director, she feared she would seem inept if an outside consultant was brought in. But she couldn't say this aloud. She knew it was self-serving, and in her gut, she also knew she could learn from Andy. She took a deep breath.

I think it's a good idea," she declared to Everco's Leadership Team. "I'm in."

"I still say it's a waste of time and money." Fred smacked his stack of paper and rattled the cups on the table.

"Easy, buddy. Well, I hate to agree with him," Richard smirked. "But he's right. The bottom line is that there's no return on investing in culture."

They had all been surprised when Richard had walked in for the meeting. Each assumed it was a coincidence that he happened to show up at the exact time of their scheduled meeting to discuss whether or not to proceed with Culture Fulfillment. Leslie had planned to call him today about his absence from work. She needed to prepare herself first, though; he had never received feedback well. She knew he didn't care much about Everco, but he always brought in the orders when they needed them. The orders weren't always the best fit for Everco, but it was work nonetheless. She hoped that his presence today meant she wouldn't need to have that conversation with him.

"Actually, Richard, there is a measurable return, as Andy explained in last week's meeting." Leslie refrained from adding: which you would know if you had shown up. Instead, she leaned forward in her chair and explained to Richard about the NPS® scores taken before and after Culture Fulfillment that showed significant increases in workplace satisfaction.

Richard rolled his eyes and seemed unconvinced. Sensing his reluctance to sign off on the investment, Hilda chimed in and told the team about the formula used in *The Culture Fix* book to calculate the ROI, or in this case, Return on Culture.

"Some companies that have implemented this program have netted a ten times or more return," she declared.

Leslie admired Hilda's enthusiasm now more than ever. Had Hilda always been this enthusiastic about Everco's culture? Or was this a new development? Either way, it bolstered Leslie's confidence at a time when she needed it most. As the Leadership Team continued to discuss returns, Leslie thought of her own hesitations about investing in culture. She knew hiring Andy would require an investment in resources and time, but her biggest concern was sustaining results once Andy left. If she failed to do so, she wondered what her employees would think and if it would make her look like a lousy leader.

But she was also curious—even eager—to hear what her employees thought. She imagined a future where she could delegate freely and spend more time with her family. She envisioned being closer to her work team and even having fun in the process. She knew it was unlikely the entire leadership team would agree; after all, had they ever all agreed on anything? Nevertheless, as she noted the excitement in her gut, she thought, I'm in.

***

"I'm so excited to get started, Andy."

Leslie felt great saying the words. The meeting with the Leadership Team hadn't ended in a consensus. It was more like a standoff. It would take some time to get the entire team on board, but she was confident in her decision. She knew it was what Everco needed, and she was beginning to understand that it was what she needed, too. She wanted to like her employees and the company they built together. She longed to feel energized and joyous when she arrived and when she left.

"I'm excited, too, Leslie."

Andy was always honored and humbled to be trusted with the noble and important work of moving teams to action, and he was particularly thrilled to help fulfill Everco's culture. Together, they talked through the contractual agreement, and Andy explained the monthly payment. "I will continue to be your partner in this Culture Fulfillment project until you are satisfied and love the results, but at any point, if you feel you're not getting value, there's no obligation. You can cancel the project, and I will turn over everything I owe you at that time, and no further payments are required. We do that because we are confident in the value we deliver, and we don't want clients to feel pressured."

Andy explained that the next step was for her to select a Culture Liaison—someone who exemplified Everco's CoreVals and was a champion of culture—to work with him each week. She chose Hilda, and he agreed that she would make an excellent Culture Liaison. Before saying goodbye, he also asked her to think of other culture czars to invite to join leaders on the Culture Team in two weeks at Workshop 1: Alive Day.

As soon as she hung up with Andy, Leslie went straight to Hilda's office. Hilda looked up from her work when Leslie walked in.

"That was quite an animated discussion earlier, wasn't it?" Hilda seemed amused.

"Was it?" Leslie replied. "I guess I'm just getting used to it." They both laughed. "That's actually why I'm here," Leslie continued. "Apathy." Hilda looked confused. "I'm starting to realize my role—my responsibility—in the culture here at Everco. I don't want to be apathetic any longer. I want to feel the culture here is alive and thriving, and I want others to feel it, too. That's why I'm going ahead with the project," she announced.

"That's great!" Hilda exclaimed.

"I just spoke with Andy, and on behalf of Everco, I'd like you to be Culture Liaison to move us through the initiative."

Hilda was honored. She had finished reading *The Culture Fix*, and she was confident that the process would work at Everco. Hilda thanked her and assured her that she wouldn't let the team down. Leslie explained the weekly cadence of calls Hilda would have with Andy and the role she would take as liaison between him and the Culture Team.

"Our first piece of business," Leslie continued, "is to choose some other culture champions to join the Culture Team."

Leslie and Hilda quickly agreed on two obvious choices: Sid and Crissy.

Sid worked in Client Services. In the eighteen months he'd been at Everco, he'd charmed clients and co-workers alike because he worked hard and was reliable. He was outgoing, and nothing ever seemed to bring him down. Those around him appreciated his unsinkable mindset.

Crissy had been at Everco for four years. She wasn't interested in a leadership position, but she held influence with her coworkers nonetheless. She was a solid designer and easily earned the respect of those around her. She was introverted by nature, but what she added to collaborative projects was invaluable. Her speech was thoughtful and deliberate, and she was always eager to tackle creative projects that challenged her. She had a growth mindset that tended to spread to those around her. Any team she was on succeeded, and it was in large part because of her.

Hilda agreed to contact Sid and Crissy and invite them to the Culture Team, but first, she emailed Andy to set up their Kickoff Call. She couldn't wait to get started.

Week One: Kickoff Call

"Hilda, thank you for taking the time to meet with me," Andy beamed at her through the computer screen. "This Kickoff Call will be the first of our ongoing weekly meetings that give us opportunities to maintain momentum and identify any areas of support you need." Andy told her the first step of Culture Fulfillment was to administer the Leadership Questionnaire and Employee Culture Survey. "These anonymous surveys help determine where leaders and employees believe we are on the culture health scale," Andy shared. "They also provide a measure of Everco's culture today that we can track over time as we progress towards a fully actuated culture."

Andy explained that he would send her links for each unique survey, spaced several days apart, that she would then distribute to leaders and employees. "I'll share results from both surveys with you next week, and we will review and embellish them in preparation for Workshop 1, where we will present an analysis to the Culture Team. Is there any other support you need at the moment?"

Hilda was reluctant to ask for support so early in the process, but she knew Andy was a trusted advisor. "Actually, Andy, I do need some help getting the Leadership Team on board. I've gotten some pushback about the surveys and their importance. Any advice?"

"Unfortunately, it does happen that not all team members are enthusiastic participants. When you do receive this kind of feedback, I encourage you to ask the person to consider Everco and all the employees who deserve a better culture. Culture Fulfillment isn't about one person; it's about all persons."

Hilda relished her new role as part of Everco's Culture Team. Not only did she have new responsibilities that challenged her, she felt she had a new purpose in the workdays ahead. Having a culture roadmap that told her how to achieve a valued culture gave her confidence and hope that Everco's people would be safe, protected, and engaged in their work in new ways.

***

When Hilda received the leadership survey link from Andy the next day, she drafted an email to share with the Leadership Team. She hoped that the anonymous survey would offer Andy and her the baseline they needed to know where and how they might proceed with Everco's Culture Fulfillment. She knew she would learn a lot from Andy and that it would prove to be an invaluable relationship for her here at Everco and beyond. She would always be thankful to

Leslie for entrusting her with the responsibility of being the Culture Liaison, and she was not going to let her down.

To: Leadership Team

From: Hilda H.

Subject: Culture Fulfillment Leadership Questionnaire

Leadership Team,

As you know, we are beginning the exciting journey of Culture Fulfillment within our organization. The first step in that process is determining how you rate our current culture at Everco. Please take a few minutes to complete the survey (link below) by Wednesday at 5 pm. This is the first of 2 surveys we will be completing this week that we will review during our upcoming culture workshop. All responses are anonymous.

Thank you.

Hilda H.

Human Resources Manager, Everco

Next, she clicked the link and took the survey herself, scored on a spectrum from "Strongly Agree" to "Strongly Disagree." Some of the questions were ones she had never thought of before—like whether or not she avoided difficult conversations at Everco. She felt a twinge of guilt marking "Strongly Agree," but she understood that she needed to answer honestly in order for the Culture Team to have an accurate picture of the existing culture. She hoped others on the Leadership Team would offer the same honesty.

Leadership Questionnaire:

For each statement, please choose from the following options: Strongly Disagree, Disagree, Neutral, Agree, Strongly Agree.

- We have a clearly defined set of core values and they are proudly and publicly displayed.

- There are 6 core values or fewer and each one is explained with descriptive behaviors.

- They feel real, unique, and specific to our organization.

- We have brought them alive with graphics, imagery, characterizations, or themes.

- Our employees and some other stakeholders could name all of the core values from memory.

- We capture, record, and memorialize our defining lore and core value stories to imbue our culture.

- I am not afraid of difficult conversations because I use the core values to empower those moments.

- We have prescribed scenario-based questions that our culture czars use to interview every candidate.

- We have a method for numerically evaluating our candidates, our employees, and our teams.

- We have a process for keeping the core values thriving through our meeting rhythm and processes.

- We have a monthly nomination and recognition process for catching employees committing core values.

- We announce the nominations, tie them to the appropriate value, and share the stories at least monthly.

- We use our core values in everyday conversation to reinforce our culture and empower our actions.

- Our core values help our leadership delegate responsibility and perpetuate accountability.

- Our employees and teams use the core values like a compass to make the same decision our leadership would in any given situation.

- I consider our CEO, leadership team, and at least some of our employees to be culture champions.

- Our CEO believes that they are leading a culture, not just a company.

- We can unequivocally say that our revenues and profits have increased as a result of our deliberate management of corporate culture.

- We have defined and communicated a measurable core purpose that defines why we do what we do.

- Our employees love where they work (culture) and why they work (core purpose).

***

When Hilda opened her email later that week, she saw a message from Andy. It was time to initiate the Employee Culture Survey. Andy reminded her to send the unique survey link to all employees, including the Leadership Team. Hilda immediately drafted her email and hit send. There was no going back now.

To: Everco

From: Hilda H.

Subject: Culture Fulfillment Employee Culture Survey

Everco Employees,

As you know, we are beginning the exciting journey of Culture Fulfillment within our organization. Completing this quick survey by Friday at 5 pm will help Everco's Culture Team get a pulse on its cultural environment and will help us initiate some improvements. It is anonymous, so please share openly. Thank you in advance for caring about Everco's culture.

Thank you.

Hilda H.

Human Resources Manager, Everco

For the second time this week, Hilda clicked a link and answered each question honestly. One question made her pause: If the company was a person, what kind of person would they be? Once again, her instinct was to gloss over the negative answers, but that would defeat the purpose. She wrote: "A well-meaning person who got sidetracked by growth and sales. A person who wants to do good work and be a good team member but is too weighed down by too much bickering to be able to take the time to see people and care about them." She wondered how other employees would respond to the same question. She didn't know how she was going to wait until next week to see the results.

Employee Culture Survey

- How long have you worked at this company?

- What would you say is the legacy of the company's founder(s)?

- If the company was a person, what kind of person would they be?

- How would you describe the corporate culture today?

- If your company already has core values, how many of the core values can you recite without looking them up?

- Do you strongly identify with our core values and believe that they define our culture perfectly?

- What do you think the core values should be? Please state any positive values that you believe apply. Remember, they must exist in the organization, not be aspirational. Why do you think these values apply?

- Which employee in the organization do you admire the most and would love to clone? Pick someone that makes you say "I wish all our employees were like them."

- Why did you pick this person? What are the qualities, attributes, and characteristics that make them valuable?

- What are some of the positive behaviors that just happen naturally in your organization? Pick ones that help the company succeed.

- What value or behavior would you love to see more of?

- Please share your favorite positive story from your time at the company - one that is a good example of the company values.

- How would you rate the overall culture at your company? Why?

- Do we talk about the Core Values enough in our organization?

- If you have established core values in the company, would you say they are alive, thriving, and being used to drive performance?

- Do you have any other thoughts that you would like to share with your leadership about the culture?

- What score would you give the company for having a great culture?

- How likely would you be to recommend working at our company to a friend?

Week Two: Coaching Call

"I'm so excited to see the survey results today," Hilda admitted to Andy at the start of their second weekly coaching call.

Andy chuckled. "I love how invested you are in this, Hilda. Shall we get started?" Andy shared the survey results across their computer screens. They carefully considered the charted results and the unique responses for each.

"We're looking for places where the scores skew high or low," Andy explained. "We want to pull some of those insights to share with the Culture Team at Workshop 1 next week. We also want to look for unique stories, jokes, and lingo that illustrate the best of the current culture and any disconnects between departments as well as larger conclusions as to why those exist. Let's also pay attention to any repeating themes and values we notice."

There were a large number of respondents who noted the lack of good culture. Most couldn't name the existing values, and the ones who could called them "merely words on the wall" or "empty."

As expected, many employees and leaders also referenced the COO's abrupt departure.

"I'm not surprised," one respondent wrote. "People don't do what they say here, and after a while, it wears you down. Raised voices and the tone of emails don't make it feel safe, either."

There were also several references to the "sales guy"— presumably Richard—who some team members didn't feel respected the work of the creative team. It also appeared that the creative people weren't motivated to do good work. One respondent admitted, "I don't give it my best, but there's no point because people don't listen, the work isn't valued, or it's overruled by leadership."

Andy shared that from his experience, one of the most important things employees want is to feel valued. "Sadly, we don't have enough of that in the workplace."

One of the phrases that showed up most often from employees and leaders was "no accountability." Andy knew that having defined values in place would help that. He understood that leaders' behavior matters and that when leaders don't keep their promises, there is little incentive for employees to do so. Everco needed solid, easily referenced values that would help peer-to-peer behavioral correction without animosity or push-back, and they needed a common, empowering language to help them sustain culture.

Andy and Hilda also made note of the responses that mentioned the chasm between employees and leaders. In fact, several employee surveys relayed asking for meetings with supervisors that continually got postponed. Andy knew the leaders weren't avoiding the employees on purpose; they were living in chaos and were having trouble finding the time. In Everco's culture without accountability, this had become a cycle—a habit even—that left employees feeling undervalued.

They chose five examples where current culture didn't align with best practices and identified five survey stories that illustrated the existing culture. Next, they calculated the average score of Everco's culture—55 percent by the Leadership Team and 47 percent by the employees—as well as the high and low scores, and added those into a presentation template Andy had prepared for next week's workshop. They talked through the details of Workshop 1 and made sure they were prepared.

When Andy asked about other culture champions who could join the Culture Team next week, Hilda told him more about Sid and Crissy. Andy agreed that they sounded like great fits and would be assets to the team.

"Sid and Crissy will be brought into the confidence of the group," Andy explained, "and will see these survey results.

Welcoming some trusted, popular colleagues from throughout the company into the early Culture Fulfillment process is a deliberate step toward building trust and fostering acceptance." Trust was something they both agreed that Everco needed to foster.

Finally, Hilda and Andy talked about the employee interviews Andy would conduct on Day 2 after next week's workshop.

"The objective is to listen and respond in an effort to dig deeper into Everco's existing culture and to test whether the values we identify during Workshop 1 resonate with employees," he explained. He asked that these be eight to twelve employees who were not on the Culture Team. Hilda said she had some employees in mind and would happily schedule those.

As they said goodbye, Andy thanked her for her time and her insights into Everco's culture. "I'm excited for us to share these results with the Culture Team next week at Workshop 1: Alive Day."

When they ended the call, Hilda couldn't stop smiling. She had never felt such purpose in her work before and knew that she was exactly where she needed—where she wanted—to be. Her hope was that soon all of Everco's employees would feel the same.

Chapter 4: Bring Culture Alive

WELCOME, EVERCO CULTURE TEAM to Workshop 1: Alive Day. I'm honored to share this experience with you."

As Andy talked through the agenda for the day, Hilda moved in her chair. She could barely contain her excitement. She'd expected to feel extraneous during this process, but instead, she felt a new excitement about her career, her contribution. Going through the survey results last week with Andy had opened her eyes, not only to the current culture, but to her role in fixing it. She wasn't surprised with the results from some of the surveys. The employees described the CEO's values as driven, visionary, serves clients, workaholic. She was also not surprised to see some of the descriptors of the current culture: not trusting, fast growth, feels difficult. Together, she and Andy had determined which results were most beneficial to the Culture Team's mission of unearthing the unique sentiments of Everco's culture.

Andy welcomed everyone by name. Before the workshop, he'd interacted with Leslie, Hilda, and Fred. He felt he'd connected with each one. He'd also introduced himself to Sid and Crissy. Sid was personable and open as always. He made eye contact with Andy and smiled freely, much like he did when Hilda had asked him last week to join the Culture Team. Crissy's response to Andy was enthusiastic too, but in her own more subdued way.

After a few minutes of chatting, when Andy felt the team was more allied, relaxed, and present, he took a centering breath. "Many organizations in crisis are there because of a failure of culture. If culture is not intentionally discerned, defined, and managed, then a default culture emerges that does not serve the organization. Equally ineffective or destructive is a defined culture that is not led, not kept alive and thriving. Then the organization misses out on the power of an environment that is led by its culture, especially in times of crisis."

Just then Richard barged in, talking on his phone. Andy smiled while Richard finished his call and took a seat beside Fred. Fred moved his stack of papers away from Richard and sighed.

Andy was unperturbed. "Richard, welcome. I'm glad you're here. Considering the investment Everco is making in culture, our time here needs to be made a priority. We are committed to showing up on time, being present, and staying focused."

Richard smirked and put his phone away.

"An organization's enduring impact and legacy begins and ends with culture," Andy shared. He explained that having an "alive" culture meant everyone was accountable, protected, safe. Teams had the capacity to withstand disruptions and offer sustenance to one another. Difficult conversations that promote healthy, safe relationships were embraced, not avoided because they were rooted in values, and the team had a language to keep behaviors within the intended culture. The right people were hired and retained, and their potential was recognized and fostered.

"Finally," he continued, "measurable and significant increases in sales and profits are credited to the ongoing cultivation and sustenance of culture." He reminded them that they would measure Everco's culture using the surveys they were about to review that tested the NPS® score of the employees throughout Culture Fulfillment and that it was not uncommon to experience 30 to 50 percent improvements in just four months. "In order to bring culture alive, we have to begin the process of unearthing it. We begin that process with surveys. You all were gracious enough to take time for these, so let's review some highlights."

Andy started with the Leadership Questionnaire. He shared that when asked how they would rate Everco's culture, the Leadership Team's average score was a 55, which meant that though they had begun the process of unearthing core values, they would benefit from investing in and fulfilling Everco's culture. Answering the same question, the employees' average score was 47. Andy explained that both numbers were low, showing room for improvement, and this discrepancy was an opportunity for future alignment.

Next, Andy displayed the results to the question: *If the company was a person, what kind of person would they be?* The team got quiet as their eyes danced across words like *harried, tired, stressed*. Andy made sure to highlight what was also before them: *determined, hardworking, cares, noble*. He reminded them that in the Alive phase of Culture Fulfillment, they are focused on unearthing the unique sentiments of Everco. "This is how we get there," he encouraged them. "By shining a light on what exists."

If the company was a person, what kind of person would they be?

tired
determined **stressed**
hardworking harried
cares noble

How would you describe the corporate culture today?

feeling **islands**
chaotic focused
connected
culture involved

On the next slide, Andy showed them responses to *How would you describe the corporate culture today?* He noted the discrepancies present from *islands* to *connected*, and from *chaotic* to *focused*. He explained that this showed the disparate experiences Everco's people had.

Andy showed the final results from the Employee Culture Survey that asked: *What do you think the core values should be?* Andy shared some of the responses that repeated, like *authenticity* and *collaboration*. He noted that many of the stories referenced were tales of teamwork and conquering projects together. Several mentioned "the backlog" a couple of years ago when teams came together to finish campaigns and meet tight deadlines. One said, "We all worked together in the conference room and had snacks and kept going until we got through the backlog. It was really incredible to see everyone come together and help to get the job done."

Leslie liked the current energy in the room. People were leaning forward, engaged in the discussion, and sharing readily. She couldn't help but notice, however, that Richard had barely participated and that Fred's posture remained closed off.

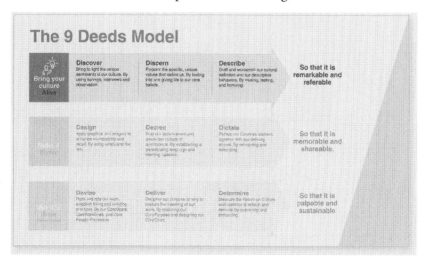

What do you think the core values should be?

creative family
integrity **authenticity**
collaboration
amazing **clients**

Andy introduced them to the "real work" of Alive Day. "In this collaborative brainstorming phase, we will accomplish 3 Deeds: Discover the unique sentiments of Everco's culture; Discern the specific unique values that define the culture; and Describe the behaviors of the CoreVals. By the end of today, you will have a unique and customized cultural description of Everco that includes core values and descriptive behaviors. This serves as a first draft that will be revisited and revised via mind maps over the coming weeks."

The 9 Deeds Model

	Discover	Discern	Describe	So that it is remarkable and referable
Bring your culture Alive	Bring to light the unique sentiments of our culture. By using surveys, interviews and observation.	Pinpoint the specific, unique values that define us. By feeling into and giving life to our core beliefs.	Draft and wordsmith our cultural definition and our descriptive behaviors. By musing, testing, and honoring.	
	Design	Decree	Dictate	So that it is memorable and shareable.
	Apply graphics and imagery to enhance rememberability and recall. By using whatsits and the "fit".	Install a commitment and create our culture of continuance. By establishing a perpetuating language and meeting cadence.	Picture our CoreVals address together with purpose defining stories. By reinspiring and reiterating.	
	Devise	Deliver	Determine	So that it is palpable and sustainable.
	Rank and rate our team, establish hiring and onboarding practices. By our Cornerstone, CoreWorkflows, and Core People Processes.	Deepen our purpose or why to capture the meaning of our work. By rediscovering our CorePurpose and designing our CorePChart.	Measure the Return on Culture and continue to refresh and reinvest. By surveying and enhancing.	

Andy explained that fulfilling culture is creative work, and the process itself reflects that. "What will that look like?" Andy asked. "Well, it might look pretty messy at first. The creative process is inherently chaotic. It isn't until later in the process that we start to see order within the chaos."

Andy told them that he liked to do a centering exercise before creative sessions to open the neural pathways between the two sides of the brain and to go within to seek what is true. He invited them to close their eyes and join him. A new calm settled in the room as they breathed slowly together and pondered the question: *What are the key values that exist in Everco that we want to come forward?*

After the exercise, Andy asked what ideas and thoughts came forward.

"Energy, zeal," Sid offered.

"Authenticity," Crissy added. "And creativity."

"Going the extra mile," Fred muttered, as the group tried not to look surprised.

Andy wrote all of the responses on the board. "Thanks for those initial thoughts. Now it's time for the first of the 9 Deeds: Discover, where we bring to light the unique sentiments of our culture."

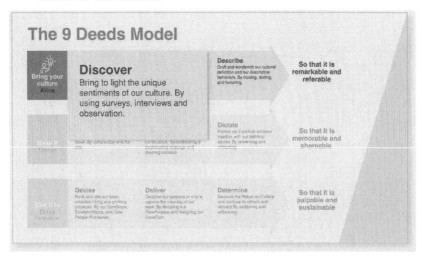

The 9 Deeds Model

Discover
Bring to light the unique sentiments of our culture. By using surveys, interviews and observation.

"Let's start with company philosophies; unique lingo, jokes, phrases; favorite stories; and best employees." Andy encouraged them to explore, to brainstorm, not to set values in stone. "We're not in a hurry," he reminded them. "Let your ideas bubble up."

Andy made four columns on a spreadsheet and captured notes as they brainstormed values associated with each one.

COMPANY PHILOSOPHIES

- Take the risk
- Trying to exceed clients' expectations
- Nobility of mission
- Renewal through service, take on too much
- Getting behind clients' missions, helping clients win and grow
- Creativity feeds the soul

UNIQUE LINGO, JOKES, PHRASES

- People time their coffee breaks when Sid does to get a "Sid fix," a dose of vitamin Sid
- Go the extra mile
- Bring your whole self

FAVORITE STORIES FROM FOLKLORE OF COMPANY

- First client. What values were there? Drive, client focus, bringing my best forward, client first. Cared deeply about the end result.
- Team collaborated to salvage a social ad campaign that wasn't working. Late on a Friday. Sid took the initiative to contact the right people, and together they solved the problem within an hour.

BEST EMPLOYEE NAMES

- Sid
- Crissy

Leslie's throat tightened. She had not expected to get emotional, but she hadn't thought about some of these stories in a long time. Hearing memories of their first client, for example, reminded her what it used to feel like. In the beginning, she was so energetic and passionate about Everco and its service to clients. It wasn't until this moment that she realized how much she missed it. How much she wanted to return to the way things felt by having the right words to describe their culture.

Moving to the next Deed: Discern, Andy asked them to continue to brainstorm values under the categories: Best Employees and CEO Values. "These are not aspirational," he reminded them. "Let's start digging. What are they?" Again, he made notes of their responses.

As they talked more about the values of the best employees, there was discussion of Sid's enthusiasm and positivity. Crissy, who was shy about hearing herself spoken of so openly, imbued reliability and stoicism. Next, they listed some of Leslie's values that emphasized her commitment and dedication.

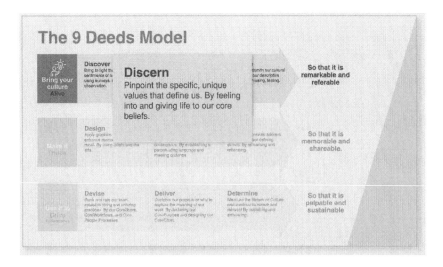

BEST EMPLOYEE VALUES

· Sid – Positivity, Enthusiasm, Zeal, Clients love, Calm under pressure, Funny

· Crissy – Hard working, Reliable, Gets it done, Stoic, Low ego, Humble, Talented, Clients like, Collaborative

OWNER/FOUNDER/CEO VALUES

· Leslie – Noble, Determined, Passionate, Visionary, Committed, Genuine, Service-minded, Inspirational, Honors diversity of thought and experience, Bold, Committed to her causes

"Okay," Andy interjected, "Now let's add meaning and context to those words. Where are the themes? What words are repeating? What trends do you see?" Andy noted their answers. "Now, from these words, let's circle our favorites with our goal being to get unique values and phrases."

Themes:

· Commitment to Causes

· Nobility

· Go the extra mile

· Collaboration

· Authenticity

· Care deeply about the end result

· Creativity feeds our soul

· Drive and Zeal

· Service-Minded, Mission-based

Andy asked Richard if he wanted to share his favorite words. Richard looked up from his phone, and it was clear he had not been paying attention. He looked at the list of words on the screen and declared, "Go the extra mile!" Then he stood and announced that in the spirit of going the extra mile, he had an important meeting to get to. He grabbed his phone and left.

Though his departure was abrupt, Andy was unmoved by it. He asked others to share unique phrases and values they saw. The team did not disappoint. They were energized and enthused. In fact, with Richard gone, the room felt lighter.

Leslie now understood—no, she felt—that Richard was a drain on the team. He was never going to be an active part of Everco's culture. Even when he showed up for things, which was rare, he wasn't present. She vowed to talk to him this week. For now, she wanted to focus on the positive. With her team around her defining the sentiments of Everco's culture, Leslie felt more inspired and energized than she had in a long time. There was an energy, and it felt right. In that moment, Leslie knew the last five years had meant something to the people in the room.

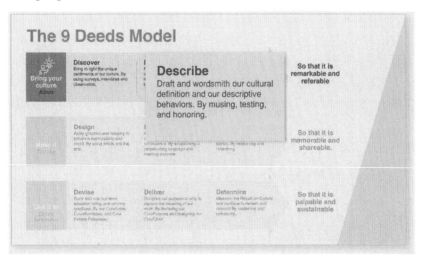

Next, Andy moved them to the final Deed of the workshop: Describe. "Let's get to the core of Everco's beliefs and words to live by. From the major values we have listed, choose your priorities. Three or four are ideal, six is the recommended maximum."

Together the team agreed on *Noble Service, Collaboration, Achieve Great Things, Deliver Results, Driven,* and *Authenticity.*

Andy continued, "Now let's think about descriptive behaviors that tell people what you mean by the core value words you have chosen. Why do we do this? To add meaning and context to the terms because as we will learn in later workshops, employees need a language to empower them and make the organization stronger. So, what behaviors describe the first core value?"

Together the team went through the values they had unearthed thus far.

CORE VALUE 1: Noble Service
DESCRIPTIVE BEHAVIORS:
We are committed.
We do great work.
We serve our clients with dignity and respect.

CORE VALUE 2: Collaboration
DESCRIPTIVE BEHAVIORS:
We think before we act.
We are kind and empathetic.

CORE VALUE 3: Achieve Great Things
DESCRIPTIVE BEHAVIORS:

We take risks.
We go the extra mile.

CORE VALUE 4: Deliver Results
DESCRIPTIVE BEHAVIORS:
We are focused on a remarkable end result.
We lead with courage.
We do the right thing.

CORE VALUE 5: Driven
DESCRIPTIVE BEHAVIORS:
We love a challenge.
We maintain a growth mindset.

CORE VALUE 6: Authenticity
DESCRIPTIVE BEHAVIORS:
We bring our whole selves.
We are fueled by creativity.

The energy in the room was palpable. Andy was practically bouncing on his feet, and Sid and Hilda joined him in standing as well.

"This is great, team. Okay, from our generated lists, which behaviors are resonating most?"

They all agreed it was a difficult choice, but Crissy chose Authenticity. Leslie admitted that Noble Service and Collaboration resonated with her most, and several others agreed. The consensus for the other two favorites were Driven and Deliver Results. Andy noted their choices and took a deep breath.

"This is really great work, team. It has been an inspiring and enlivening session. I have covered all I wanted to cover with you today. I'll be conducting employee interviews tomorrow to test some of these values and behaviors, and then I'll work with Hilda to go over those highlights, reflect on today's work, and continue moving Everco toward a valued culture. I thank you all for your time and energy."

Workshop 1: Day 2

"What was the highlight of yesterday's workshop for you, Hilda?" Andy had finished the last of his interviews with eight Everco employees, and he was eager to hear Hilda's feedback.

"Just being in the room, really. I hadn't felt that kind of... camaraderie here before, and it rekindled something in me. You see, I know what a good culture looks like—in fact, I left one for Everco—but I didn't know how to get us there."

Andy was glad he could offer Hilda and the Everco team a roadmap to Culture Fulfillment. He asked her if she had gotten any feedback from other Culture Team members.

She told him that several had mentioned liking the Everco stories that were shared, including Leslie. "I think it was good to be reminded about when we had worked well as a team." Hilda smiled. "I think everyone is excited to have unique core values and to know what they stand for."

As usual, Andy was inspired by the energy Hilda brought to the meeting. The employee interviews had gone well, and he knew Hilda was anxious to discuss his findings. First, he showed her the questions he asked.

Employee Interview Questions:

How long have you worked here?

What is your role here?

How do you like working here?

What do you like about working here?

What don't you like? How would you improve that?

How would you describe the culture here?

What are the Company's core values?

Do they ring true for you?

Tell me a story that you have heard involving a customer...

Anything else to tell me? Suggestions?

What score would you give the company for having a great culture (Max 10)

What would make it a 10?

Do the following values fit Everco's culture:

- Authenticity

- Noble Service

- Collaboration

- Driven

- Deliver Results

He opened his notes and gave her some highlights from the interviews. "The good news is that there was broad appreciation for, and agreement with, the attributes we came up with in the workshop yesterday. But I heard about some frustrations, too."

He told her that several people sounded jaded about not having their work and opinions valued, and several others shared that they didn't feel it was safe to speak up. "And when they do, they don't feel like anyone is listening to them," he explained. "It seems that the answer to many of Everco's problems is to work harder and longer. That feels unsustainable to me." Andy looked more serious for a moment. "Hilda, as you probably know, you're going to lose some more good people if things don't change."

Hilda sighed. She knew this was true. Some employees were even brazen enough to do their job searching from work.

Andy sensed her frustration and met her eyes. "But remember, one of our Post-Culture Fulfillment goals is to

Employee Interview #3: In one of my first weeks with the company, I was having a problem on a Friday afternoon with an important project due on Monday. I mentioned it in a casual conversation with a team member, and they stayed late to walk me through the problem and gave me great insight into why things were working the way they were. I learned a ton that day from the kindness of a team member.

Employee Interview #5: This summer an employee had a flood in his house and coworkers came together to collect donations and bring snacks/food over to his house for the work crew, and even kindly helped with clean up!

Employee Interview #7: The first time I "broke" something in the system, everyone reacted with genuine kindness and encouragement. My teammates helped me to understand how to correct my error while going out of their way to point out some of their own mistakes they had made in the past. This has made such a significant impact on the way I approach my role going forward.

ensure that we have a culture where people want to stay."

He shared some highlights from the interviews, specifically three that were compelling.

"What stands out to me from this selection, Hilda, is the recurrence of kindness. This isn't a common value I hear about, and it didn't come up in the workshop yesterday. Yet it is clearly something that exists within Everco, and this is why we conduct interviews in addition to surveys and workshops. To find those important but less obvious values. Kindness in a workplace can be a real competitive advantage."

Next, he shared with Hilda that several employees mentioned feeling out of touch with the Leadership Team and wondered what the overall goals of the company were. He assured Hilda that this was common and that in Workshop 2, he would suggest to the Culture Team that they hold monthly all-company town halls. "This will help all employees better understand what Everco is about and trying to achieve."

Andy explained that they would use these stories, along with all of the results from their brainstorming sessions, to create mind maps, which would include potential core values and descriptive behaviors. "Later, we will add stories to these to create the CoreVals address for the Launch Event. For now, though, we just want to reflect on what we discovered at Alive Day." He said it would be helpful if they both made mind maps independently and then brought them together at next week's coaching call.

Hilda appreciated the much-needed step-by-step plan to guide her through this process. Each day, she grew more excited and more empowered to step into the role that had been gifted to her.

Chapter 5: Make it Thrive

HILDA WAS NERVOUS ABOUT creating a mind map from the early values the Culture Team had unearthed at the Alive Workshop. When she shared her hesitations with Andy, he assured her that the values and descriptions would evolve over the weeks of the Culture Fulfillment project. "The final draft will likely differ from your first draft, so don't feel pressure to produce something special right away. Just reflect on what came up in the workshop. Trust the process."

That week, the two refined and developed an initial draft of the mind map. Hilda then shared it with the Culture Team and relayed the feedback to Andy during their next coaching call.

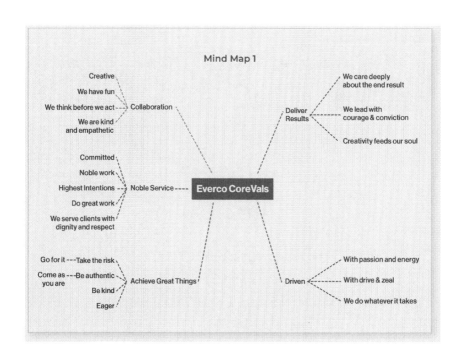

She was proud to report that the Culture Team loved the initial cultural description. "Even Fred liked it!" she laughed. "Several people did point out, however, that *Noble Service* and *Collaboration* seemed to have some overlap."

Andy and Hilda decided to combine those two values and then further refined the descriptive behaviors.

The next week, Hilda presented the refined cultural definitions with the team, but this time, they had mixed reactions.

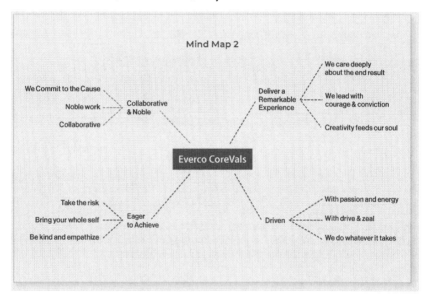

On the next coaching call with Andy, she explained their reservations. "Though everyone like the combining of Noble Service and Collaboration, some people didn't like the value Driven," Hilda reported. "They said it's too conventional and doesn't represent our special magic. What do we do now?"

Andy told her he was grateful for the feedback because they now learned that value was not resonating with the team. It was time to dig deeper into the work. Andy said they would return to their notes from Workshop 1, as well as the stories they gleaned from employee interviews. "This is an opportunity to choose a stronger value that we may have overlooked."

Hilda looked back at her notes and found "go the extra mile." She explained to Andy that though it captured the idea behind *Driven*, it might better resonate with the team.

Andy agreed, and they revised the mind map to reflect the new language.

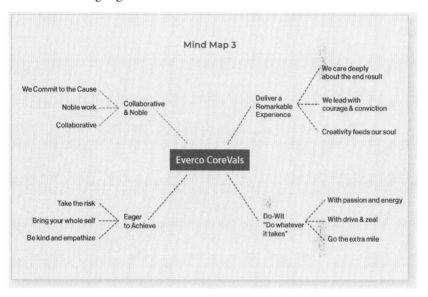

That week, in addition to iterating mind maps and reviewing them with the Culture Team, Hilda also initiated and reviewed the Client and Vendor Poll results to present at the upcoming second workshop. Before sending out the polls, Hilda admitted to Andy that she rarely thought much about the downstream effects of their culture on clients and vendors. She knew the poll results would be valuable and wondered how they might continue to shape the core values they had begun to unearth.

Workshop 2: Thrive Day

It was the morning of Workshop 2, and Leslie was ready. Over the last month, as she'd reviewed and reflected on each week's draft of Everco values, she'd explored how she wanted to show up as a leader and how she might embody the values they were defining. Since then, she had committed to the daily practice of being a strong, centered leader who was more attuned to the importance of her own demeanor. She was working to truly *see* her employees, just as Andy had championed when he explained the concept of *Sawubona*. In doing so, she reclaimed the joy of her work, and she saw— truly saw—the burgeoning enthusiasm of her team.

As she settled into a conference room chair, she thought about how her own priorities had shifted over the last several years. She realized she had been chasing the "growth god"—and always pursued every bit of business, whether it was in her and her teams' best interests or not. Some of that she credited to her entrepreneurs' group that glorified growth above all else. Thanks to Andy's teaching, however, she realized that, unless aligned to purpose, growth in itself wasn't actually valuable. In fact, accord-

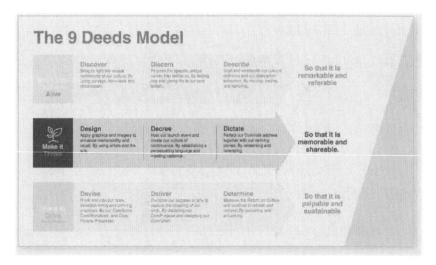

ing to Andy's experience with other companies, he assured her that once she invested in Everco's culture and aligned herself with clients who held similar values, they would grow without force. It was for this reason that she was relieved to learn that Andy would start the workshop with the results of the Client and Vendor Polls. She didn't know how much longer she could wait.

After Andy warmly welcomed the Culture Team and walked through the day's upcoming agenda, he turned his attention to the polls.

"These are tools we use to determine what values Everco's clients and vendors see in our organization and how they feel when they interact with our teams," Andy said. "In fact, these observations might be the most real of all the behaviors we have discussed." He explained that they had polled fifteen clients and five vendors, and interviewed three of the polled clients and three of the polled vendors. He noted that he was most interested in the client relationships that were working well—Everco's best clients—because those were the dynamics he wished to replicate. He displayed some sample questions he asked the outside groups.

Sample Client and Vendor Interview Questions

1. What do you consider to be the marketing message or positioning statement of the company?

2. Why do you choose to partner with this organization?

3. What benefit does the company provide to your organization?

4. What is their character? What kind of company are they?

5. What values do you observe when you interact with them?

6. What feeling does it give you to work with the company? (confidence, trust, ambivalence, concern, etc.)

7. How likely is it that you would recommend this company to a friend or colleague? (1-10.) Uses the NPS® score.

8. Are there other observations you could share with us about the culture or values of the company?

"If you'll notice, early questions are to get them talking," Andy explained. "Then I build up to what feelings they feel and what values they see our team demonstrating at Everco. The intent and sequence of these questions is to increasingly lead the client or vendor towards using more emotive answers, words and phrases that could inform our values-based cultural definition."

He shared that when he and Hilda had reviewed the results earlier in the week, they'd looked for common threads, new values that hadn't been revealed during their culture work thus far, concepts to probe during client interviews, and for confirmation that the identified values were

Client Interview Results

What values do you see Everco represent?

✓ Client #1: Relational, personable, responsive, kind, always taking feedback = I LOVE that clients matter. They try hard but there seems to be some frustration in getting things done.

✓ Client #2: They respond quickly, which I appreciate, but they don't always have the answer right away, particularly regarding deliverables from other team members. Going through some changes, direction not super clear, it's as though they are working on reducing bottlenecks.

✓ Client #3: I like working with the creative and support teams. Even during challenging times, they are responsive, which makes me feel that they care at least.

indeed recognized by clients and vendors. He displayed several responses they had deemed most relevant.

"What stood out to Hilda and myself was the repetition of a value that first showed up in our employee interviews: kindness. This confirms that this value isn't just an internal one but is also extending beyond the company to the client. Another common answer was responsiveness. Though we had not yet identified it as a value, it is clearly something that Everco's clients recognize and appreciate. As such, Hilda and I added that to our cultural definition notes." Andy showed

---

Client Interview Results

How does working with Everco make you feel?

✓ Client #1: I feel heard and like I'm an important part of the team. I like helping them grow. They always used to work hard and really care about the work they delivered but lately I'm not having a consistent experience. Some teams seem better than others.

✓ Client #2: I feel like the people are confident. They make me feel safe and that they've got my back. They are super responsive when I need them. Ultimately, it's always a great end result.

✓ Client #3: They are always reasonable, and they come back with helpful information. They are proactive, and they don't just give the easy answer. It's mostly been a positive experience, and I am pleased with the quality results, but it does seem some of the newer employees were hired in a rush.

---

them the next question as well as key responses.

Andy highlighted some of the more unique feedback, specifically that *responsive* showed up again as well as new values—*results* and *experience*. "I suspect those words would not have come out of employee interviews. If we hadn't done these polls, we wouldn't have understood some of Everco's unique competitive advantage. We are learning that, when we recruit, we want to find people who embody *kindness and responsiveness*, are *results-oriented*, and care about the client *experience*. Take being responsive, for example: Isn't that a marvelous value? Everyone appreciates a fast, caring response, so the more we can hire people who are responsive and the more we keep it front-of-mind for employees, the better the experience for our clients and the stronger our culture and competitive advantage." Andy explained that some of their upcoming work would be to train new employees and coach existing employees on what those traits look like.

"For example," he continued. "We want Everco employees to know that when they are staring at a full inbox, they need to prioritize emails from clients who require an immediate response and do it naturally."

Next, Andy displayed highlights from the Vendor Poll.

Vendor Poll Results

✓ Vendor #1 Research Firm: Gets a different experience with each department. Likes working with creative departments best because they do what they say and are highly responsive. This really helps us do our job.

✓ Vendor #2 Qualitative Research Company: Doesn't feel there is cohesion around what the company is trying to do. Sales team is too rigid. Likes the creatives because they can have fun getting it done.

✓ Vendor #3 Ad Placements: They take on too many customers and then push the demand to produce down to us. Doesn't feel like a true partnership.

Before Andy could even point it out, Sid announced, "There's *responsive* again!"

"That's right," Andy said. "It's clearly a value that clients and vendors appreciate. We want to make sure we capture that." Andy explained that when a company's values are aligned with clients and vendors, business is smoother. "You naturally make more money and have fewer problems when aligned. If not aligned, friction causes inefficiencies, and you lose money because everything is harder. When we rank Everco's best clients against our CoreVals, they score well. This is a great way to determine which clients you want to build your business around and which clients you don't."

Andy asked Hilda if she would like to say more about the discovery she made while reviewing vendor interview results.

"Sure," Hilda said confidently. "As I was reading the responses to Andy's questions, I noticed that the vendors all referenced the ease they felt working with Everco's creative team. They felt there was a cohesion there, and that they were easy to work with." Hilda asked if anyone was surprised by this.

Sid spoke first. "I'm not surprised at all. In fact, most of the time that I speak with clients, they first ask to speak with Crissy!" Everyone laughed, including Crissy.

"That's great!" Andy exclaimed. "Let's dig deeper here. Sid, why do you think they want to talk to Crissy?"

Richard joked that it was because Crissy had been there since the beginning.

"Well, there's some truth there, Richard," Crissy responded. "The reason is that I've made a lot of connections since I've been here. You know, when Everco first started, it was all about the creative departments. We weren't as enamored by sales then. We had a more involved role with clients. And we all shared a mission. Because it's a noble one!"

"Come on, now," Richard retorted. "There is no creativity without sales! It's what drives Everco."

"It's certainly not as simple as creativity versus sales," Leslie interjected. "It should be about bringing in the right clients at the right pace to allow us to provide more creative value to clients and thus expand their spend and renewal rate."

As the group discussed quality of sales versus quantity of sales, Richard got more agitated.

"Give the sales department one week off and see how creative you are," he railed. "Without clients, there is no reason to be creative. Let's not forget that."

Andy took a centering breath and calmly reminded the team that these are the moments when cultures are defined and brought to life.

"The emotions you feel right now? That's culture in action. You all are so passionate about Everco, and we see that in these conversations. The opportunity here is to discover a value that clients and vendors have appreciated for a long time that we have perhaps overlooked. But before we move into brainstorming what that value may be and how these results might inform our work, let's take a moment to center ourselves."

As he had done in the first workshop, Andy asked them to join him in several minutes of simple breathing in a mindful way with their eyes closed, ruminating on the question: *What other value exists in Everco that we want to come forward?* Afterwards, he asked them to share what came up.

To the surprise of all, Fred spoke first.

"I've been here since the beginning, too," he shared. "It's been long enough to know the people who work here. I think our clients and vendors see the same thing that drew me here five years ago. And that's our noble mission."

Fred proceeded to tell them how he had known Leslie since she was a child. How he had worked with her mother decades ago when Leslie, barely a teenager, started working at her mother's not-for-profit.

"Like her mother, Leslie has a nobility of character that's rare. When she decided to open her own firm five years ago,

I was the first to join her because of the good she wanted to do for the world through Everco."

When he stopped talking, the room was silent. Rarely had Fred ever shared this much of himself, and he had never spoken of his personal history with Leslie.

Andy beamed and jotted down some of what Fred shared.

"I completely agree," Crissy contributed. "I, too, have always felt pride about Everco's work serving not-for-profits." She also shared that she had always felt supported by the creative team and appreciated their positivity. "You can't be negative around that team. They won't have it! If you're negative, they make you go outside and ground."

Leslie had never heard of this. "Ground? Do you all do this often?" she asked.

"It started out as needed," Crissy replied. "But then it became a daily event. We meet under the big Blue Spruce in the side lot. We started calling it 'Spruce Your Blues.'"

Leslie was shocked. She felt excluded that she'd never been asked to join, but then again, would she have agreed to sit outside under a tree with her employees?

"I go, too," Sid admitted. "Really, I invited myself. I just wanted to breathe a little and be outside. Things sometimes get so serious here, you know?"

"It's a job," Richard reminded them. "It's supposed to be serious."

Fred laughed. "I don't remember you being so serious at Everco's picnics!"

Now Richard laughed, too. "Ah, yes, those were the days." He looked at Andy and explained that they used to have monthly picnics. "We had a battle of the bands, homebrew beer tastings, and even a karaoke contest."

When Andy asked if they still had picnics, Fred shook his head. "It got too expensive. And participation started to wane when we grew fast and hired quickly. We stopped a couple of years ago."

"Those sound amazing!" Sid exclaimed. "Can't we start that up again?"

The team laughed, and Leslie thought about how it wasn't just that the picnics got expensive. The truth was that they used to like working together and spending time together. She wanted to bring that back—not just the picnics, but the enjoyment of their connections.

As if reading her mind, Andy shared that when you create a valued culture, you like who you work with, and you're more inclined to spend time together—whether in the office or under a tree! "Now that we have some new insights on the CoreVals and descriptive behaviors from the client and vendor polls, let's prepare ourselves to shift focus by engaging in another centering exercise."

As he had done before, Andy asked them to take a series of slow breaths together. When finished, Andy smiled and welcomed them to their fourth Deed: Design.

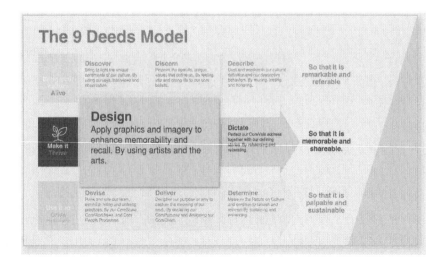

Andy began by sharing that 65 percent of people are visual learners. He displayed a quote by Stanford University's Robert E. Horn on the importance of combining words and visuals to create a visual language.

"This is why creating graphic, image-rich displays for your core values and their descriptors is a must. Unless Core-Val words are highlighted in some graphic way and hung on

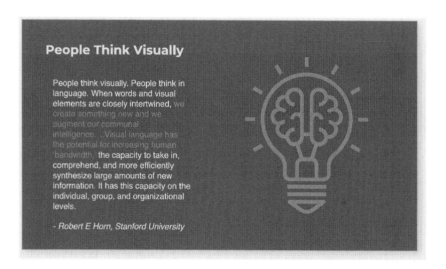

People Think Visually

People think visually. People think in language. When words and visual elements are closely intertwined, we create something new and we augment our communal intelligence. . . Visual language has the potential for increasing human bandwidth, the capacity to take in, comprehend, and more efficiently synthesize large amounts of new information. It has this capacity on the individual, group, and organizational levels.

- *Robert E Horn, Stanford University*

the wall, they really don't exist and aren't part of the culture. Simply having them in an email or on the company intranet is not effective. We like to see CoreVals on posters, pocket cards, and put in front of everybody in creative ways via desktop wallpapers, mouse pads, coffee mugs, or other everyday items—especially if it's pertinent to Everco. A jigsaw puzzle that employees can build over lunch in the break room is another great example of how to display values. Keeping CoreVals hidden suggests the company is not proud enough or serious enough about them."

Next, Andy displayed their current CoreVals and descriptive behaviors.

CORE VALUE 1: Collaborative & Noble Service
- Descriptive Behavior 1: We commit to our causes.
- Descriptive Behavior 2: We choose good work with good people.

CORE VALUE 2: We Only Live Once
- Descriptive Behavior 1: We bring our whole selves.
- Descriptive Behavior 2: We have fun and go for it.

CORE VALUE 3: Deliver a Remarkable Experience
- Descriptive Behavior 1: We respond promptly.
- Descriptive Behavior 2: We lead courageously.

CORE VALUE 4: Go the Extra Mile
- Descriptive Behavior 1: We feel the joy of creativity.
- Descriptive Behavior 2: We pursue growth.

"Now let's focus on themes, images, and company histories to make our values come alive." He started with the first category: Personas/Themes. He asked if they could conceive of a set of characters, existing ones or original ones, who embodied the core values. If personas didn't work, he suggested selecting a theme that evoked imagery, like the ocean, or outer space.

Sid spoke first. "The theme that is resonating with me is something to do with nature."

"That's what I was going to say," Crissy and Hilda said at the same time. "What about the rest of you? Does a nature theme resonate?"

The others nodded in agreement.

"That's why most of us live here," Fred added. "Because we all love the outdoors. This is one of the most beautiful places on earth. No matter where you are in town, you're only a few minutes away from hiking trails, vistas, and rivers and lakes so clear you'll weep. In fact, if we didn't have to be inside, most of us wouldn't be."

"That's great." Andy clapped. "Let's brainstorm what nature-based images might fit each value."

The group first talked about images representing the four elements or the four directions. They expanded on this, discussing true north and the imagery of a compass. Andy made notes capturing ideas.

"This might be odd," Crissy added. "But I keep seeing an image of my horse, Trusty."

Andy encouraged her to say more.

She explained that when she thought about the descriptive behaviors—of being committed, collaborative, serving—it reminded her of training her horse.

"Trusty is always ready, willing, and helpful. She never complains. Whether we need her to ride or pull, she is up for the task and will do it all day. She had to learn that I never ask her to do anything dangerous or harmful. I feel like we do noble work together in nature and move along at the pace of peace."

"At the pace of what?" Leslie asked.

"At the pace of peace. It's just a saying that my partner and I use to remind ourselves to move at Trusty's pace. It means the organic pace that she's comfortable with, not our own hurried pace."

"I love that!" Leslie exclaimed. "At the pace of peace! That reminds me of our work with clients. Sometimes we have to match their pace—or the project's pace—rather than rush though it at the pace we'd prefer." Leslie asked Crissy if they could borrow that language.

"Sure," Crissy laughed. "Now that you mention it, Leslie, training horses and handling clients are way more similar than I'd realized."

The group agreed to work *at the pace of peace* into the descriptive behaviors.

"Well, I wonder if Trusty can inspire an image, can my beloved Kokanee Salmon?"

Sid spoke up. "Fred, can you say more for those of us who don't hit the rivers every weekend?"

Fred laughed. "Well, maybe you all should! You can learn a lot from fish. Salmon in particular have amazing journeys, living the first few years of life in our cold, deep lakes before migrating upstream. Their appearance even changes during their migration, and their bright silver gives way to a deep red. It's amazing. When I think of *going the extra mile*, I think of salmon—those tough, strong fish readying themselves for their wondrous journey each fall."

Leslie was still surprised by the evolution she'd witnessed in Fred. She had known him for most of her life, and he had always seemed hardened. The past several weeks, however, he'd shed something and seemed lighter, freer. Maybe Everco was more of a burden on him than she had realized. She supposed it was naïve to ever think Everco's haphazard culture had only affected her. It was clear that the entire team felt freer.

"I love it." Leslie smiled. "I think salmon would be a wonderful image for *going the extra mile*, and it is certainly unique to Everco and our people."

Fred seemed pleased as the team brainstormed other animals that might fit the remaining values. Ultimately, they decided an eagle was a good image for *we only live once* and a mountain lion represented *deliver a remarkable experience.*

"These are some great ideas, team," Andy encouraged. "Now, let's move from images to talking about music." He explained that theme songs were a great way of rooting the culture in memorable ways that leveraged the arts and the left brain. He suggested the song be used to kick off Everco's monthly Town Hall meetings. "We won't finalize this today, but let's capture any early ideas we have. We will officially kick off a theme song competition at the Launch Event."

"I only have one request." Richard smirked at Fred. "No Conway Twitty."

The team laughed, including Fred, who explained to Andy, Sid, and Hilda that he used to end every family picnic with a Conway Twitty tune. "I just gave the crowd what they wanted," he joked.

The team continued to brainstorm songs, amused by the generational divides it revealed among them.

"Great job!" Andy said when they were finished. "Now, let's talk about how we will display these images. Where will you put your main CoreVals posters, for example? What collateral will you use to display CoreVals and imagery? Such as website, advertising, packaging, pocket cards, flyers, key fobs, costumes, and more?"

The team came up with some unique ideas, like having some items relate to the outdoors—compasses, water bottles, scenic puzzles, and hiking sticks.

Leslie chimed in, "Maybe we can get a special bridle made for Trusty since she inspired our imagery!"

"She can be our mascot," Sid added. "Maybe she can even join us at our next picnic?"

As the team discussed Sid's idea, Leslie smiled. She loved hearing the team *assume* there would be a picnic soon. And that they would attend. She was so grateful to be here, with these people, in this room, talking about this topic. *Is this what it feels like to like who you work with, where you work, and why you work?*

Andy turned and spoke directly to Leslie. "The moment you announce your core values to your team is the moment when you will accept the privilege and responsibility of being a leader—not just of a company, but of a culture that extends well beyond the company. Before that moment arrives, however, you will want some assurance that you will be heard and that your message will be well received. That type of respect and faith is rooted in trust."

As they moved into the next Deed: Decree, Andy explained they would establish that level of trust through periodic meetings that establish goals, deliverables, and deadlines. The upcoming Launch Event would be the initiator of a new meeting framework—one in which Everco would

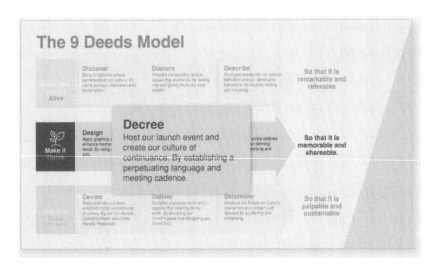

discuss and address issues in light of the company's values and purpose.

Together, the team planned the ongoing meeting rhythm that allowed current and future employees to get comfortable using Everco's cultural definitions and provided them with a new cultural language. Andy reminded them of the employee interviews that referenced feeling disconnected from the Leadership Team.

"In an effort to keep all employees aligned with Everco's mission, I suggest monthly all-company townhalls." He also suggested incorporating values into weekly team meetings by beginning each one with shout-outs—opportunities for one employee to recognize another's behavior that was tied to a value. He introduced them to Notice & Nominate—a formalized scheme designed so employees could nominate one another for significant behaviors tied to company CoreVals. He mentioned Catch & Correct—a mechanism they would return to during the Post Launch Prove & Improve cycle for handling behaviors that are out of line with values.

Next, they moved into the final Deed for Workshop 2: Dictate.

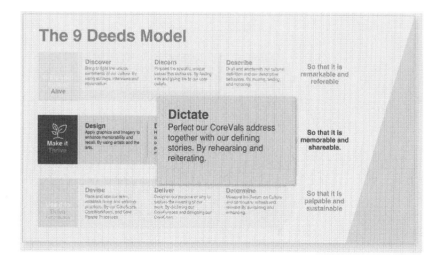

They discussed the details of the Launch Event and determined which team member would speak about each value. Andy explained that over the next several weeks, he and Hilda would develop a presentation deck to be used. In the meantime, he encouraged Leslie to begin work on her Core-Vals Address and offered his assistance if needed.

"The next step is an exciting one. Hilda and I will set up a competition with our designers to create a core values infographic that includes values, descriptive behaviors, and visual icons. The goal is to arrive at a custom design motif for each value as well as collage when they are all brought together. Most companies use outside designers or crowd-source potential designs, but we are lucky enough to have these in-house."

As they concluded the workshop, Andy thanked everyone for their ideas and enthusiasm. Then he offered a final reminder. "This is a good time to point out that distributing these items and displaying our CoreVals poster is not the end; it's the beginning."

As they all said goodbye and moved to their next tasks, Leslie found herself energized and repeating, 'It's only the beginning.'

Chapter 6: Use it to Drive Performance

WHEN LESLIE ASKED HILDA if she wanted to have their morning meeting while walking outdoors, Hilda thought it was a trick question.

"I just thought it would be nice to get outside and get some steps in," Leslie said with a wide smile.

She was right. It was a beautiful day, so clear and crisp you could see each peak of the surrounding mountains.

Once they were outside, Leslie declared, "This is why I live here." She exhaled deeply. "The air. The sun. The colors." She paused and then asked, "Why did you move here?"

"For Everco," Hilda answered. She shared with Leslie about her last job several towns away. "I loved it there, but it was small, and I wanted to take a leap for my career. I really felt like I could do more than I was doing there."

"Well, you certainly can! And you're proving it." Leslie stopped walking. "I'm serious, Hilda. You are doing an amazing job with our culture. I could not have done this—we could not have done this without you. Thank you. Truly."

Hilda was thankful for Leslie's encouragement. "I do believe in Everco, Leslie. And I do believe what we're doing is working."

They started walking again and talked some more about the hope and energy they were feeling in their interactions with others. Their conversation flowed easily between work life and personal life, and when they returned to the office, they each felt energized for the workshop.

Hilda looked at the culture notes spread across her desk.

Since the last workshop, she and Andy had finalized the mind map and CoreVals. The values and the descriptive behaviors felt authentic and unique to Everco, and she knew the Culture Team felt the same. Together they made sure their Core-Vals checked all the qualities of a great set of core values:

- Not too many for easy recall
- Unique so they feel special and exclusive to the organization
- Catchy and therefore easy to use in everyday conversations
- Supported by descriptive behaviors or sub-texts to provide context
- Both overlap and tension exists between the values to ensure balance and applicability

It was when she and Andy were testing Everco's Core-Vals against this list that Andy also mentioned that acronyms could provide an additional layer of coolness and usability.

"As always happens when one trusts a creative process," Andy explained, "unique features emerge such as acronyms." He pointed out that Deliver a Remarkable Experience could be shortened to DARE and that the other values also had acronyms that worked to varying degrees. With this realization, Hilda agreed they should adopt them as part of the definition. She could see them being used as shorthand for the wordier versions of the values and becoming part of Everco's distinct cultural language

Since then, they had gotten the Culture Team's approval on the acronyms and had also seen two rounds of designs and provided feedback before choosing a winner.

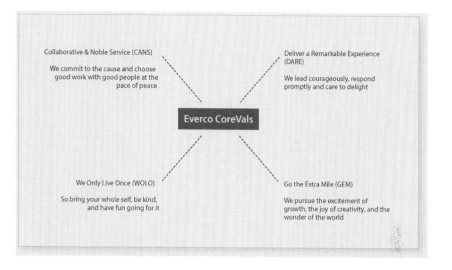

Collaborative & Noble Service (CANS)

We commit to the cause and choose
good work with good people at the
pace of peace

Deliver a Remarkable Experience
(DARE)

We lead courageously, respond
promptly and care to delight

Everco CoreVals

We Only Live Once (WOLO)

So bring your whole self, be kind,
and have fun going for it

Go the Extra Mile (GEM)

We pursue the excitement of
growth, the joy of creativity, and the
wonder of the world

Also in the weeks since the last workshop, Andy had introduced Hilda to the CoreScore, a tool for hiring, unhiring, and evaluating based on CoreVals. Together, they'd drawn on company lore and the stories the team shared earlier to come up with scenario-based interview questions and answers. These general and role-specific questions would help Everco probe for personal values and ensure alignment of future hires. She hoped the team would agree that these were ways to use their CoreVals to drive Everco's performance.

She gathered her notes and a cup of tea and headed to the conference room. She knew that if she hadn't been part of the process—and hadn't had the privilege of leading it—she would hardly be able to explain the alchemical process she'd seen and felt during Culture Fulfillment. Thankfully, the outputs of the process would allow others to share that sense of excitement at next month's Launch Event. But first, she was excited for the Culture Team final Workshop: Drive.

***

After their centering exercise and a lively discussion on what success at Everco could look like, the Culture Team was energized to continue the collaborative, iterative work of Culture Fulfillment.

"As you all know, Hilda and I have been working together throughout this process to further hone and iterate on the work done in these workshop sessions. I'm proud to show you the result of that work—a draft of Everco's CoreVals poster complete with initial images."

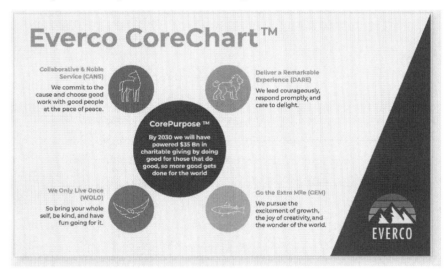

The team discussed how the images worked with the values and behaviors. They captured their feedback to relay to the designer, and then Andy moved into the first Deed of the final phase.

"Our task is to Devise practices and strategies to harness our CoreVals that will ultimately drive Everco's performance to new heights. We will rank and rate our team, establish hiring and unhiring practices, and draft our CoreWorkflow—

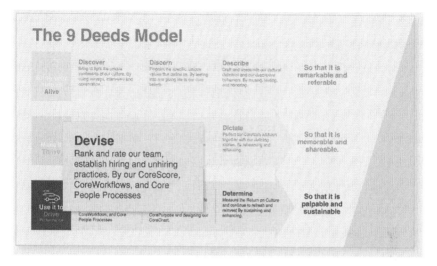

where we bring together values and the way that work flows through the company."

This is what Leslie felt most excited about—when theory was applied to drive results. She and Hilda had been meeting regularly to talk about ways to hire, unhire, and evaluate to preserve the core values. She wanted to ensure that they designed and documented the fundamental work Everco did in line with the ideals they had worked hard to unearth. She knew she could only keep the values alive and use them to drive Everco's performance if she could bring both together and set people up to succeed within the operational framework. She trusted Andy and Hilda, and the entire Culture Team, to do this. She also noted, with some amusement, that she had adopted Andy's use of *unhire*. As he had explained early on, the word *fire* put all the responsibility on the person being unhired; but to be fair, the company and hiring individual must also bear responsibility. She preferred thinking about it as an uncoupling, not a firing, and it set a different tone for her.

Andy explained that Core People Processes were the hiring, unhiring, and evaluating protocols based on CoreVals. "With these goals in mind, let's start with the hiring process," Andy continued. "Hilda and I composed questions that Everco will use for all prospects during the interview process. We drew on company stories shared in our workshops as well as employee interviews to come up with scenario-based questions that require potential employees to answer with specific events rather than generalities. We want to get to the emotions behind the circumstances because those emotional responses are tied to personal values. Let's take a look."

As Andy noted the team's feedback to the questions, Leslie wondered which employee's home flooded. How had she not known about this? And what did it say about Everco's culture? She felt proud in a new way, not just because of the successful business she had built but also because of the character her employees displayed—in and out of the office. Well, most of her employees. There was still the issue of Richard.

She thought this workshop was one last chance for him to get involved, but he sent her an email last minute that he wouldn't make it. She wasn't surprised, but she was angry and eager for Andy's teaching on unhiring in line with culture. She had avoided that difficult conversation for years, but she wouldn't any longer, not now that she had a way to score for cultural fit as well as a language for the unhiring conversation.

She turned her attention back to Andy, who was explaining the CoreScore—a numeric measurement that indicates the degree to which employees and teams work in concert with CoreVals according to an objective scale.

"It's important to have a methodology for measuring fit with culture, whether we are assessing an employee, a team,

Everco Culture Stories	Source	Value Shown	Interview Question
In one of my first weeks with the company, I was having a problem on a Friday afternoon with an important project due on Monday. During one of my scheduled meetings with a team member they walked me through the problem and gave me great insight into why things were working the way they were. I learned a ton that day from the kindness of my team.	Employee Survey	We Only Live Once (WOLO)	As a manager or coworker, have you ever been asked for help? How did you respond?
The first time I "broke" something, everyone reacted with genuine positivity and encouragement. My teammates helped me to understand how to correct my error while going out of their way to point out some of their own mistakes they had made in the past. This has made such a significant impact on the way I approach my role going forward.	Employee Survey	Go the Extra Mile (GEM)	Tell me about a time when you made a mistake or were asked to help correct a mistake. How did you handle the mistake?
This summer an employee had a flood in his house and coworkers came together to collect donations and bring snacks/food over to his house for the work crew, and even helped with clean up!	Employee Interview	Collaborative & Noble Service (CANS)	Have you ever experienced a coworker needing help like in this story? What did you or your company do and what did you like or not like about it?
I feel like the people are confident. They make me feel safe and that they've got my back. They are super responsive when I need them. Ultimately, it's always a great end result.	Client Interview	Deliver a Remarkable Experience (DARE)	Tell me about a difficult project you or your team experienced. What did you do to ensure a remarkable experience for your client?

a client, a vendor, or even a candidate for employment. The CoreScore is a perfect tool to do this, and one that removes some of the subjectivity. We all have feelings about these entities, whether we acknowledge the feelings or not, and this tool can make it very clear very quickly what the appropriate course of action is.

"The fastest way to change culture is to change some of the people. First, we need a way to measure; then we need a way to respectfully remove, or unhire, people when they don't fit the team to preserve the harmony and greater good of the group," Andy said. "They will also help you acknowledge superior work without bias."

Leslie felt her shoulders relax. She had only recently realized how much pressure she carried, and she was trying to let it go. Being a CEO was a beautiful burden. Though she would always carry the weight of being a leader, being able to trust the team and processes they established gave her the breathing space she needed.

One value of the CoreScore, as Andy shared, was that it easily applied to both current employees and new candidates vying to join the team. A low score suggested the candidate in question was not a great fit; whereas a low score for a current employee meant they either needed to be coached or unhired. It was like a litmus test that created trust and built a culture of accountability. It also eliminated the guesswork from interviewing prospects and evaluating staff performance and provided an objective scale, showed trends, and got more accurate over time.

"By assigning a red, yellow, and green status to the Core-Score, it quickly becomes evident who your rock stars are—in green, who needs feedback or to be provided with training—in yellow, and who needs to be unhired or not considered for employment—in red. Scores that are less than ideal do, however, provide the opportunity for introspection and culture-powered conversation. How about we give it a try? Any volunteers?"

Sid's hand shot up. The team scored him against each of the CoreVals and weren't surprised to learn he was a strong culture fit. Then they proceeded to score one another against each of the CoreVals. It was a moment of vulnerability for them all, but they had created a trusted community within their team, and they understood it was an important checkmark for Everco's culture. Scoring Fred as a group felt awkward at first, but he soon made it easy for everyone by participating in the conversation and accepting the scoring. He didn't feel threatened and had nothing to lose by acknowledging that he was at the end of his career and not the best fit with the updated cultural definition of a company that was in transition. His attitude helped the Culture Team grow into a healthier, more open and trusting cohort.

CoreScore™

Everco	CoreVals				Total	Key:	
CoreScore™	Go the Extra Mile	Collaborative & Noble Service	We Only Live Once	Deliver a Remarkable Experience	Individual CoreScore	Team member demonstrates this value:	
Sid	3	3	3	3	12	All the time	3
Leslie	2	3	2	3	10	Most of the time	2
Hilda	3	2	2	2	9	Some of the time	1
Crissy	3	2	3	3	11	None of the time	0
Fred	1	2	2	2	7		
Richard	1	0	0	0	1	R/Y/G	Action
						High Correlation	Nurture
Candidate 1	3	2.5	2	2.5	10	Average Correlation	Train
Candidate 2	1	2	0	2	5	Low Correlation	Unhire
Best Customer	3	3	3	3	12		
Worst Customer	1	1	0	0	2		

When they were done, Leslie looked at Richard's row on the chart. There it was. What she had known for years but hadn't had a way to test. Red. Weak fit.

Andy sensed a sudden heaviness in Leslie's demeanor, and he intuited that it had to do with the CoreScore of some of her team. He asked them if they could take a break, and most headed for the door to refill mugs and grab fresh air. Leslie stayed behind, lost in thought.

"It's common to have a few 'reds' in the mix," Andy said to her. "The CoreScore makes it really clear and validates whatever feeling you had in your gut about an individual, especially when benchmarked against a group of peers."

She nodded in agreement. "But then what?" she asked. She had always resisted this part of her job.

"Then it's only fair to give these individuals immediate feedback in a personal conversation, referencing the Core-Vals. They are probably not feeling comfortable in the culture anyway because they don't fit and won't feel like a valued member of the group who is making a meaningful contribution. After you give feedback, quickly decide if they are capable and willing to become more aligned, or if you need to make the decision for them. In some cases, those who are poor fits self-select and exit on their own."

That would be great, Leslie thought. In fact, if she were being honest, that was what she had been waiting for with Richard.

"Your CoreVals will help you make the tough calls," Andy encouraged. "And using the CoreScore will ensure that you do so without personal bias. Once you have unhired the low scores, you'll notice a palpable turnaround in the dynamic and wish you'd done it sooner. Companies achieve this all the time. When they do, it feels amazing, teamwork is effortless, and the company is cranking on all cylinders. All that is left to do then is to hire some high-scoring fits and hang on for the ride."

This was certainly Leslie's goal. Wherever she looked across the company, she wanted things to be going well, and people to be enjoying their work. Her mother had always said that a business succeeded through disciplined action. Winging it could not be sustained. She hoped that following standard procedures that tied into Everco's CoreVals would be an easy way to instill discipline and accountability in her staff.

Once the team returned from their break, Andy couldn't help but expand on the effectiveness and simplicity of the CoreScore tool. "Don't forget that the CoreScore can be applied to teams and other entities, too. When reviewed as a team, how does the marketing and sales team compare to the standard we have set? Or how does one client team compare to another client team? We have certainly seen how the clients observe differences in the team they are working with, haven't we? Let's apply this to our best and worst customer right now."

Five minutes later, the room was in stunned silence. They knew that MustGo was a difficult customer, but until now they had not realize how obvious it was that they needed to unhire a client, too.

Next, Andy gave them a new challenge to consider. "There is no point in building a high-performing team and then sabotaging them with crazy business goals, nonsensical procedures, or clumsy, undocumented workflows."

He said it was great people on a great team, working within an efficient, documented, and well-planned business process, that were the keys to productivity. If Everco wanted to set people up for success, he said, they needed the Core People Processes they had already discussed and a CoreWorkflow—the overarching company workflow or master process.

Andy displayed The Culture Fix Academy's CoreWorkflow as an example.

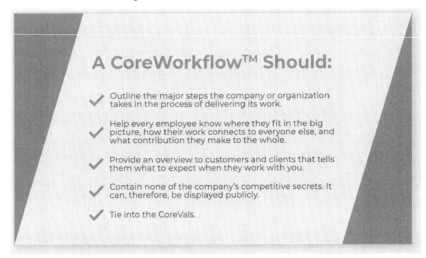

A CoreWorkflow™ Should:

✓ Outline the major steps the company or organization takes in the process of delivering its work.

✓ Help every employee know where they fit in the big picture, how their work connects to everyone else, and what contribution they make to the whole.

✓ Provide an overview to customers and clients that tells them what to expect when they work with you.

✓ Contain none of the company's competitive secrets. It can, therefore, be displayed publicly.

✓ Tie into the CoreVals.

"Do you see how this model outlines the major steps the company takes delivering its work while at the same time tying into the CoreVals? This is a powerful way to let employees know how and where they fit, and it also provides an overview to clients of what they might expect when working with Everco. Of course, all CoreVals apply across all teams, but it can be instructional to determine which value predominates for which team and in which part of the workflow."

Once the team outlined the ten steps that made up the end-to-end process of how work flowed through Everco, they summarized each step into a word or two and grouped them under reasonable departmental headings. Next, based on what they now understood about the importance of visual images, they added graphics to depict momentum.

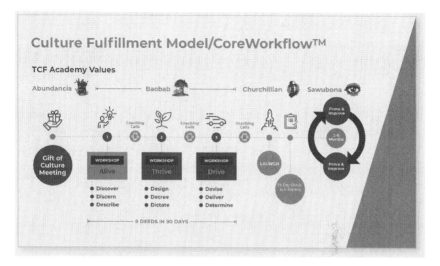

"This is great work, team! These CoreWorkflows allow us to stay on top of speed, cost, and quality metrics that are an important part of running our business and allow us to invest in creativity."

Andy asked if they were ready to move to the next Deed: Deliver.

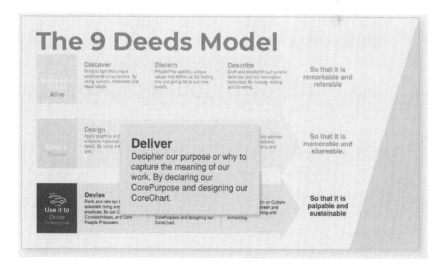

Andy explained this was perhaps the most important part of a cultural definition because it would capture the purpose or 'why' and put words to the meaning of the work at Everco. He explained that a CorePurpose not only put words to the why, but also consisted of a date and a target or measure that quantified the deliverable—the good that the company would do for the world. He called this the CoreTarget and explained that all three elements were important in order to create motivation for teams.

He displayed a series of questions that would help them define their CorePurpose and CoreTarget. He said the first three questions were reflective because they provided context and continuity to what Everco did now and where it was going next. His clients felt it easier to determine their forward-looking purpose—their CoreTarget—by beginning with where the company started.

"Numerically, it also makes the CorePurpose more exciting," Andy explained, "because the value of Everco's future deliverable is higher by including what you have already produced. Also, because your company has grown, the scale of your future deliverable value is likely going to be significantly greater, and this can really motivate everyone."

Sid asked if a purpose can be just as powerful without quantifying it. Andy explained that unless they picked a specific numeric goal to be achieved by a certain date—typically three years—they would never know when they had achieved their purpose, and the team would not be able to quantify the meaningful contributions they were eager to understand.

Andy walked them through the questions that dealt with the past and the present before turning to their future targets.

"Think of Everco's CoreTarget as the value you're giving to the world. It's a vision that will help the Leadership Team figure out what they need to build a strategy. Essentially you create a vision and then work backwards to create a strategy."

Everco CoreTarget Calculation	2021	2022	2023	2024-2028	2029	2030	Notes
Offices	1	2	3	...	9	10	National to International
Employees	100	120	144	...	430	516	< or = 10% Admin
#3 Person Teams	38	48	60	...	240	303	Each team cares for 3.3 customers (ave)
Clients	100	145	190	...	460	505	Services to SaaS platform
Ave Everco fee spend by client	100,000	108,000	116,640	...	185,093	199,900	
Revenues	10,000,000	15,660,000	22,161,600	...	85,142,790	100,949,734	Cumulative
Cumulative Revenues (10 Yr)				...		489,202,266	
Client Budget/ Funds (Ave)	10,000,000	10,800,000	11,664,000	...	18,509,302	19,990,046	100 clients w Fund of $10M ea to 500 clients w Fund of $20M
Funds impacted by Everco	1,000,000,000	1,566,000,000	2,216,160,000	...	8,514,278,967	10,094,973,367	Assuming 25% fundraising and admin costs
Funds distributed for good	750,000,000	1,174,500,000	1,662,120,000	...	6,385,709,225	7,571,230,025	
Cumulative Funds Distributed (10 Yr)				...		35,940,169,937	35 Bn in distributed funds for good over 10 years (round down)

Together, the team created a visionary number, and with Andy's help, filled in the strategies that would get them there. When they were finished, they had a CoreTarget that would help them determine how many teams, clients, and offices they needed, in addition to the revenues and budgets they would abide by. They determined that they could impact $35 billion in charitable funding over a ten-year period. It was surprising how a simple spreadsheet that laid out the key components of a strategy over time informed the path to their CoreTarget and quantified the good that they would do for the world. They would know when they got there and could track and be motivated by their progress towards the goal. Every time they delivered another campaign, won another client, or opened another office, it would all be tied to the purpose and provide meaning to their collective actions. The plan also projected that they would naturally increase the average spend of their clients; in fact, it would double over ten years as clients grew and they added larger clients.

"We have answered many questions today and made great progress," Andy encouraged. "But there is one question left. The last question, why, is the most important."

He explained that a company's purpose acted as a blanket term for consistent forward movement around mission and motive. He called this the CorePurpose—the overarching company goal and reason for being. "Having a clear starting point and well-defined idea of what success for Everco looks like conveys clarity to employees and clients. Knowing why you are in business will lay the groundwork needed to list and articulate the purpose upon which all behavior in the company will be based."

Andy explained that determining a CorePurpose was an integral step in the shift from simply having core values to truly having a valued culture, providing a legacy from which to build and develop a solid culture.

Not only would purpose provide a legacy from which Everco could build and develop a solid culture, it also would tell employees what they were working toward and why, motivating and energizing them along the way. Once they were able to spell out their CorePurpose, Andy assured them, their employees were sure to have a newfound reason to believe in what they were doing, and why they did it.

"We are humans with feelings, a fact often ignored by organizations in pursuit of more corporate goals," Andy said, showing them research on well-being. "But ultimately all that matters is the way we feel. And if we feel good in our

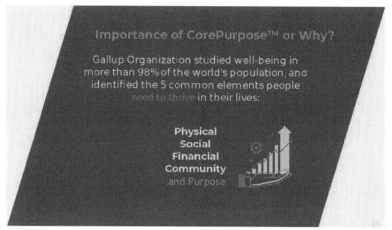

work, with our teams and about our organization, all efforts become aligned and extraordinary results are achieved. In short, employee experience drives customer satisfaction."

Leslie knew this to be true, but she had struggled with getting to a defined, measurable purpose for their business—one that spoke to the why and addressed all the components that she wanted to see and present to her team. She knew she wanted to put "words to her why," and she was, once again, thankful that Andy offered them a tool for these more nebulous aspects of business.

"Though the why might be one of the most important aspects of business, it is also one of the hardest concepts to decipher and put into words."

Importance of CorePurpose™ or Why?

"People don't buy what you do.
They buy why you do it."

- Simon Sinek, *Start with Why: How Great Leaders Inspire Everyone to Take Action*

He shared a quote from one of his favorite books on the subject.

Andy noticed that each person in the room was engaged and present. He felt once again the noble intentions of Everco's Culture Team. He encouraged them that in order to get to a defined, measurable purpose for Everco, they needed to get introspective on why Everco's clients bought their services.

"Why do they buy what you sell, and how does it benefit them? The why should be about them and not about you or Everco. You need to think about your value to your client's customer. Then you are aligned to your client's CorePurpose and have the same motives they have, which will propel your conversations and your collective success."

After a few quiet moments of centered breathing, Andy turned to the group and asked what fundamental good Everco did for the world. The answer should apply to all Everco clients, he reminded them.

"Well," Leslie offered. "Since our clients are not-for-profits, several house the homeless, one increases art programs for at-risk youth, and others help with job training and placement for incarcerated adults. When I think of it that way, Everco facilitates so much good in the world."

Andy asked the team how their clients thrived.

Fred answered, "By having healthy income stream from donors, individuals, corporations, fundraising events. We essentially run campaigns which increase donations."

Andy pushed back. "Why do they come to Everco? What good are we doing?"

"We increase availability of services that benefit the disadvantaged," Hilda added.

"Ah." Andy smiled. "But why?"

"So donors can feel that their own abundance can be shared," Hilda responded.

Before Andy could respond, the entire team called out "Why?" in unison.

"So that more good gets done in the world," Leslie answered definitively.

There was a hush in the room as Leslie's words settled on them all. That was their purpose, and they could all feel it.

"So we do good work for those who do good work so they can do more good" Sid offered.

The team agreed, and after more thought and conversation, they also defined Everco's CorePurpose: *By 2030, we will have powered $35 billion in charitable giving by doing good for those who do good, so more good gets done for the world.*

Andy had helped decipher many CorePurpose statements, and this one had a nice ring to it. Sometimes the CorePurpose "why" was so instructional, so core to the company's activity, that it became their tagline, too. After all, it is the company's reason for being. Why not use it to inform their marketing message, too? And extend the culture to the point that all stakeholders can feel what the employees are feeling? Would Everco's tagline become "doing good for those who do good?"

Leslie's face brightened. "I can see that knowing one's purpose is pivotal to the culture and to the success of an organization. How many of our clients are missing this crucial tool? We know that not-for-profit organizations have three indispensable 'customers': the clients they serve, the donors who support them, and the volunteers or staff members who help get the work done. How powerful would it be to put words to their why for the motivation of these entities to accept, donate, and give?"

"Are you considering a new product offering, Leslie?" asked Fred.

"I am," she said. "And it may be our most important yet. Sid, how would you feel about spearheading such a venture for us?"

Sid did not need to answer. His smile said it all.

With that, Andy moved into the final Deed of the day—Determine.

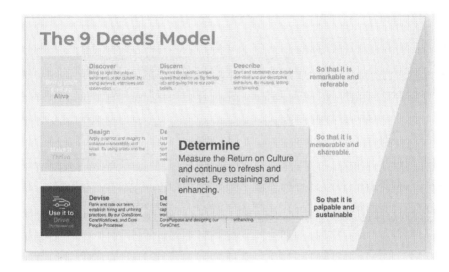

Andy reminded them of what they had discussed when they met at the Gift of Culture meeting—that building culture was the lowest investment/highest return initiative they could bring to their company. Implementing a cultural plan was less expensive, less risky, and more personally rewarding than venturing into new markets, new products, or the next marketing campaign.

Leslie understood that part of the purpose of measuring the condition of Everco's culture was to follow the return on her investment. Now that they were in the Drive phase of Culture Fulfillment, she had a clear picture of the extent of her contribution. She was also getting a sense of the exponential dividends she would receive. She was already feeling that peace of mind, better focus, more time, and less worry for herself were already worth the effort. Then factor in greater employee engagement, increased productivity and innovation, and an improved image with their clients, and she could see where increased satisfaction met higher revenues. She was glad she hadn't fretted over the intangible rewards and instead embraced them. They had led to real, measurable improvements for her business.

Andy said that with any investment, they needed to measure their return. So far, they had used NPS® scores and CoreScores as metrics, but he wanted them to be aware of another measurable—Return on Culture (ROC).

He displayed a formula for measuring ROC.

Fred shared that when they started this process, he'd been skeptical.

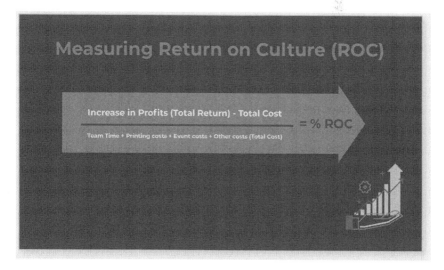

The room broke into laugher, and Sid joked, "Yeah, we all picked up on that, Fred."

"Well, I think I had good reason to be skeptical. Culture is so…intangible. I didn't think there was any way to measure it. You've really won me over with this formula, Andy."

"I'm glad you're connecting with this," Andy mused. "This is certainly speaking your language. I want to introduce you to this formula now so that we can be filling in the relevant numbers over the next few weeks. When I return for our Prove & Improve session, we will calculate Everco's ROC."

Andy shared other ideas for building in cultural measurements, like adding employees' CoreScore to their files and discussing core values during evaluative meetings. He suggested they administer the CoreScore twice a year, average those scores into a company score, and report that in order to measure the company's cultural rating and trend over time.

He also reminded them that he would be returning quarterly to survey employees to see how response changed—or remained the same—over time. Finally, he listed several ways to schedule data collection and analysis, some being as simple as performing a gut check on how the culture felt.

"This data will show you how to drive culture so that it drives your business," Andy assured them. "When everything is moving in synchronicity, you will notice improvements in team and company performance. Once you add up the numbers, you'll be able to see how well your cultural efforts drive your business toward success."

Fred asked several questions about the role of financial reports in the analysis. As Andy answered, Hilda took extensive notes. She knew that quality and quantity assessments were her tools for keeping her finger on the pulse of Everco's

Other Ways to Measure Return on Culture (ROC)

- Employee Interviews
- Periodic Surveys

Data Collection & Analysis
- Import financial and goal achievement reports for analysis.
- Compile CoreScores and survey question results from employee annual evaluations.
- Keep count of the number of monthly award nominations received.
- Facilitate consultant interviews of staff and compile results.
- Do spontaneous testing of team members and record results.
- Perform gut checks on how real the culture feels.

culture, and it was a job she took seriously. More data would give her a richer picture of the complex workplace dynamic that was culture. Identifying measurable results would give direction on how to proceed, based on what was working in their culture.

Andy's voice got serious as he brought their teaching to a close.

"Few elements of doing business are more important than a culture that includes top people performing to their full potential, in a tight team that is meeting or exceeding its goals— and having fun doing it! In addition to creating an atmosphere where you want to go to work every day, great culture is your greatest business asset. Get it right, and success will follow."

At the conclusion of the final workshop, the team applauded. Andy congratulated them on completing the final Deeds. He explained that he and Hilda would continue their work to prepare for the Launch Event and finalize the Core-Workflow, CorePurpose, and CoreChart. He reminded them that the next time they reconvened would be at the Launch Event, which was an exciting moment for all employees to be reminded that they were an integral part of Culture Fulfillment. Though there was much work for the team between now and then, he could tell that every person in the room was engaged, excited, and inspired. He was honored to have the privilege of moving this dynamic team to action.

Chapter 7: Launch

LESLIE STEPPED UP TO the front door of Everco and paused. It wasn't long ago that she'd stood in the same spot, dreading what awaited her inside. Today, she felt excitement and hope. It was Everco's Culture Fulfillment Launch Day, and she could not wait to share the process and outcome with the entire company. Five months ago, she'd felt detached— from her company, her family, her purpose. Since then, she had learned that it didn't pay to be in a frantic mode doing everything herself. By bringing the best out of her people through Culture Fulfillment, her business was more aligned, which had created a ripple effect in her life. She was connecting again in her family and friends, her physical health, even her mental and spiritual wellbeing.

She opened the front door of the company she had poured herself into for the last five years and heard laughter. Rather than head straight to her office and shut the door as she used to do, she followed the sound and found the Everco team mingling around plates of fruit and bagels in the breakroom. When she entered, Crissy called out a chipper Good Morning and handed her a cup of coffee.

"This smells good," Leslie said, inhaling deeply. "What is it?"

"Honey cinnamon latte," Crissy replied. "From the bees in my yard."

On a recent lunch hike together, Crissy had shared about her love of working her land. Leslie had caught the light in Crissy's eyes when she talked about her days with her partner, cultivating the soil, building a life. Since that time, Crissy had begun working from home one or two days a week. Less commuting allowed her more time to care for her farm animals and achieve the balance that was so important for her. It made Leslie think of Andy sharing the Zulu greeting sawubona—"I see you." Since then she tried to take time to fully "see" the people she worked with each day. To cultivate those relationships. To show up and take opportunities to connect with them. She wanted to make sure that she made her employees feel as though they were at the right place, working with the right people. She was also reading a lot about conscious leadership and starting to model what she was learning.

The team sipped their lattes and joked that Everco should start beekeeping. Leslie felt joy hearing her team make plans—if only jokingly—to be with one another. *On purpose.* Leslie was proud of what she'd built and even prouder of how the team had restored it during Culture Fulfillment. As she sipped her latte and laughed at Fred's impression of wearing a bee suit, Leslie felt it: *There's no place I'd rather be.*

***

Leslie thanked the Everco team for being at Launch Day—whether in-person or remotely. She shared the afternoon's agenda and then introduced the Culture Team. She also welcomed Andy and explained his role as the Actuator who'd moved the Everco team to action and helped them rediscover their essence as a group. She invited him to say more about Culture Fulfillment.

Andy stepped up and beamed.

"This is an exciting moment in Everco's evolution. The reason we call this Culture Fulfillment is because we didn't create a culture. We already had it, and now we are fulfilling it. That's why we put so much effort into surveys and interviews and getting input from all of you, because we're not trying to capture who we want to be. Rather, we're trying to capture the best of who we already are… and build on it."

Andy explained that during their time together, they would look at some high-level results of those surveys and then follow the path the Culture Team had forged to discover and discern Everco's unique values. But first, he shared what having a "good culture" means.

"When we have a great culture, first and foremost, everyone loves where they work, who they work with, and why they work. Everyone is accountable, and the core values help us have a language for holding each other accountable. Peer accountability is marvelous, but so is bottom up accountability. The core values will power us through this. CoreVals keep everyone in alignment, which means we are better positioned to make decisions the same way the leaders would. Perhaps one of the greatest benefits is that core value wording can help us enter into difficult conversations with others. They provide a framework that can ease some of the discomfort and help us maintain a healthier environment."

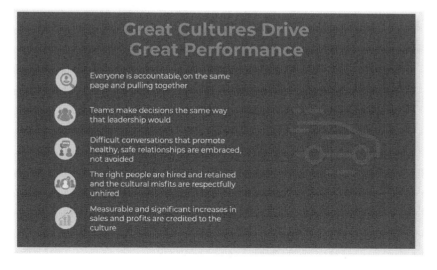

Great Cultures Drive Great Performance

- Everyone is accountable, on the same page and pulling together

- Teams make decisions the same way that leadership would

- Difficult conversations that promote healthy, safe relationships are embraced, not avoided

- The right people are hired and retained and the cultural misfits are respectfully unhired

- Measurable and significant increases in sales and profits are credited to the culture

He shared that Everco had unearthed a culture using the Alive, Thrive, and Drive model.

"First, we brought culture Alive by discerning definitions that made CoreVals easily referable. Next, we made it Thrive with graphics and art so that values are memorable. Then, we used it to Drive performance and make the culture palpable and sustainable. But what matters most is what we do next."

He explained that the process, including this Launch Event, were the fun parts.

"Starting today is when the work begins. What matters is what we do with the Gift of Culture. Who do we share it with? How do we pass it forward? In order for it to be a gift and remain a gift, we must use it as such."

Andy paused, and the room stilled.

"It's about a valued culture, not simply core values. We brought the culture alive by being intentional with the words we chose for our cultural definition; we made them thrive by talking about them every day and having nomination and correction schemes; and we use them to drive performance by using them in hiring and measuring ourselves according to the values."

Next Andy shared the Employee Survey results with them, which always got people's attention. He explained how visuals could often be more effective than words and displayed the word chart that populated the words that were most used in the text responses to the question: *If the company was a person, what kind of person would they be?* Andy highlighted some of the words like *determined, hardworking, cares, noble.* He reminded them that in the Alive phase of Culture Fulfillment, they were focused on unearthing the unique sentiments of Everco. "This is how we get there," he explained them. "By shining a light on what exists."

> If the company was a person, what kind of person would they be?
>
> tired
> determined stressed
> hardworking harried
> cares noble

On the next slide, Andy showed them responses to *How would you describe the corporate culture today?* Just as he had done with the Culture Team, he noted the discrepancies present from *islands* to *connected*, and from *chaotic* to *focused*. He explained that this showed the disparate experiences Everco's people had and allowed the team to address those gaps.

> How would you describe the corporate culture today?
>
> feeling islands
> chaotic focused
> connected
> culture involved

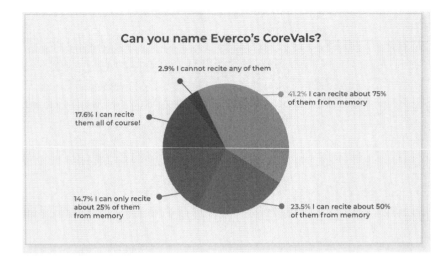

Next, he moved on to highlighting other notable results from the Employee Survey, like the fact that most Everco employees had trouble naming the initial values. He explained they would avoid this same pitfall by incorporating images and graphics into the newly drafted values, which they would see in a moment.

But first, Andy wanted to share the results of the question: Do we talk about CoreVals enough?

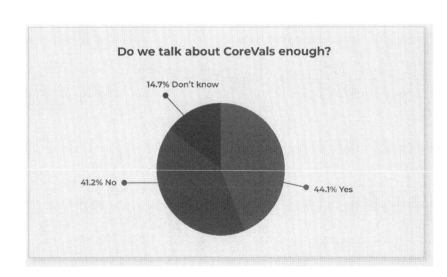

"When I see this chart, I get excited because it's an invitation to bring CoreVals to the forefront. Employees share that they want leadership to talk about the values more and lead from a place of caring." Andy explained that the Culture Team had put forth some exciting ideas on how to do this.

When Andy moved on to Client and Vendor Polls, an Everco employee asked why they would poll external people if they were trying to discern internal values.

"That's an excellent question," Andy encouraged. "We poll them because we want to know what values our best customers see us demonstrating. It's our goal to make certain that the culture retains the values that our clients and vendors appreciate and that we leverage those for competitive advantage. That's how we keep the partnerships we have and gain new ones. Want to know what clients and vendors said about you?"

The room laughed when there was a mixed response to Andy's question. He displayed his findings, and just as he had done with the Culture Team, he highlighted the value of responsiveness.

Client Interview Results

What values do you see Everco represent?

✓ Client #1: Relational, personable, responsive, kind, always taking feedback = I LOVE that clients matter. They try hard but there seems to be some frustration in getting things done.

✓ Client #2: They respond quickly, which I appreciate, but they don't always have the answer right away, particularly regarding deliverables from other team members. Going through some changes, direction not super clear, it's as though they are working on reducing bottlenecks.

✓ Client #3: I like working with the creative and support teams. Even during challenging times, they are responsive, which makes me feel that they care at least.

The chatter in the room grew as participants got more engaged in the process. Andy turned the presentation back over to Hilda to explain the Culture Fulfillment journey. She shared the steps the Culture Team took to discern Everco's culture, starting with the feedback from the surveys.

"We unearthed the core values that are present within Everco," Hilda explained. "Over time, we turned those into mind maps. Next, we took a close look at the words that we considered for our values, our potential future CoreVals, and we further broke them down to describe what they mean to us, called descriptive behaviors, and how we see them lived out every day. This process helped us feel confident that the values that we chose were the best values to describe who we are. The new ones are quite different from the hackneyed ones we picked years ago. Once we discerned the values, we worked to bring more meaning to those values by adding statements that show exactly how we live out each value through our behaviors. After that work was finished, we discussed ways to visually represent our values, because research shows that when we combine words with imagery, we increase our recall and augment our communal intelligence. Adding images brought the words alive."

Next, Crissy stepped up to speak and presented the first value: Collaborative & Noble Service (CANS). She shared that the idea of nobility and collaboration were values first mentioned in the employee surveys and developed further during interviews. She read the descriptive behavior for the value and relayed the employee story that exemplified it. She even showed them a photo of her horse Trusty, who had inspired the image for the value. "So, can we live up to this value?" she asked her peers. "Yes, we CANS!" she concluded.

CoreVal #1: Collaborative & Noble Service (CANS)

✓ We commit to the cause and choose good work with good people at the pace of peace.

Employee Story: "This summer an employee had a flood in his house and coworkers came together to collect donations and bring snacks/food over to his house for the work crew, and even helped with clean up!"

EVERCO

It was Sid's opportunity to present the second value: We Only Live Once (WOLO).

"This next value is one that is important to me. Life is too short not to be filling up the days with laughter and kindness. Others at Everco feel this way, too."

Sid shared the descriptive behavior of the value and the story that was first unearthed from an employee. He also displayed the image of the eagle chosen to represent the value.

"We felt that an eagle, known for its opportunistic behavior and majestic appearance, represents this value. Because of its recovery from being an endangered species, it also represents how, when we work together, bringing our whole selves, we can make miracles happen. Like the eagle itself, we want to continue to protect this value so that all employees are free to be themselves—and have fun doing it! So, here at Everco, it's not YOLO, but a more inclusive WOLO!"

It was Hilda's turn to present the third value: Deliver a Remarkable Experience. She shared that this value seemed especially pertinent to her role at Everco, especially when

CoreVal #2: We Only Live Once (WOLO)

✓ So bring your whole self, be kind, and have fun going for it.

Employee Story: "In one of my first weeks with the company, I was having a problem on a Friday afternoon with an important project due on Monday. During one of my scheduled meetings with a team member they walked me through the problem and gave me great insight into why things were working the way they were. I learned a ton that day from the kindness of my team."

EVERCO

considering its descriptive behavior—We lead courageously, respond promptly, and care to delight. She told the group how this value was unearthed by the client interviews Andy had conducted.

"Though we had not yet identified it as a value, we uncovered that our clients recognize and appreciate our responsiveness. This not only enhances our workplace, it offers up a competitive advantage. In short, at Everco, we DARE to deliver a remarkable experience!"

CoreVal #3: Deliver a Remarkable Experience (DARE)

✓ We lead courageously, respond promptly, and care to delight.

Client Story: "I feel like the people are confident. They make me feel safe and that they've got my back. They are super responsive when I need them. Ultimately, it's always a great end result."

EVERCO

Fred stepped up to present the final value: Go the Extra Mile (GEM). He read the descriptive behavior and shared that this value was originally discovered as company lingo during a brainstorming exercise and then later reinforced by employee stories like the one displayed here.

"I never thought I would see the day that I got to stand before you all and talk about fish, but here we are." Fred chuckled and explained that the salmon was the chosen image for this value because of the amazing journey it takes during its life.

"A salmon is not afraid to venture into a new environment—leaving its safe, deep lake to swim upstream in search of possibilities. When I think of going the extra mile, I think of salmon, and I think of you all here at Everco—tough, strong creatures readying yourself for growth, creativity, and this wide, wondrous world. You all are real gems, and GEM is our fourth and final value!"

Leslie stepped in front of the group and took a centering breath as she had watched Andy do each time he spoke—not because she was nervous, but because she understood the significance of the moment and of her role at Everco.

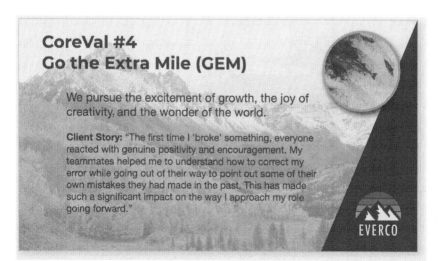

CoreVal #4
Go the Extra Mile (GEM)

We pursue the excitement of growth, the joy of creativity, and the wonder of the world.

Client Story: "The first time I 'broke' something, everyone reacted with genuine positivity and encouragement. My teammates helped me to understand how to correct my error while going out of their way to point out some of their own mistakes they had made in the past. This has made such a significant impact on the way I approach my role going forward."

EVERCO

"After hearing more about the values unearthed at Everco, I have one question for you: does this sound like a place you would like to work?"

The employees cheered and clapped, and the Culture Team exchanged smiles.

"This all sounds pretty great, huh? Do these values feel like who we are? And who we want to continue to be?"

The Everco team applauded again, and Sid let out a loud cheer.

"Fantastic," Leslie continued. "I will share that one of the most important parts of this journey for me was defining our CorePurpose."

She explained that a company's purpose is the overarching company goal and reason for being. "It tells us what we're working toward and why, motivating and energizing us along the way. We now understand that feeling engaged in our roles makes us like where we work and who we're working with. Core values are great, but at the end of the workday, we all want to feel like we've done something meaningful for the world. That's why we wanted to be really specific about naming our 'why'—our CorePurpose—and putting a number on it—our CoreTarget. That way, we are working towards a vision and can better track our way there."

Before she displayed Everco's CorePurpose, she recapped how they had determined it by asking themselves a series of questions and continually drilling down to why it mattered.

"Ultimately, we realized that Everco grows those who grow others so that they can grow, too. In order to be more specific, however, we wanted to put a number on that. I'll let our resident number guru explain that."

Fred chimed in and explained that by answering a series of questions about future targets, they were able to build a vision and then a strategy to get there. "Adding this together with our CorePurpose really helped us determine the value that Everco brings to the world. Would you like to see it?"

The crowd cheered.

Everco's CorePurpose

✓ By 2030 we will have powered $35 billion in charitable giving by doing good for those who do good, so more good gets done for the world.

EVERCO

After a few moments of silence, the employees began clapping again. They were engaged and lively. Leslie felt a swell of pride to be here with this group of people, sharing Culture Fulfillment.

Fred stepped before the audience again and cleared his throat. He explained that as many of them knew, he hadn't been on board with Culture Fulfillment at first. The room chuckled.

"It didn't seem necessary," he scoffed. "But then, something changed, and it seemed the most necessary thing there ever was. It's hard to explain, but you know I'll try!" he laughed. "But the more we talked about Everco's culture and worked to intentionally define it, the more connected I felt to the people here and the good work we do."

He shared that one of the defining moments in his epiphany was in the drafting of the CoreWorkflow, which illustrated how work flowed through the company and how Everco's values were threaded through that. Fred displayed the image and walked through Everco's workflow, tying each step to a CoreVal.

"It is a polished, high-level overview with graphics, values, and CorePurpose to put in front of clients. It's a sales and marketing tool that shows them what to expect when they work with us."

The audience was quiet, eager. Hilda stepped up to explain that all of these components added up to Everco's CoreChart—an infographic that combined their CoreVals, CorePurpose, and CoreTarget.

Sid started a drum roll on the desk. The others joined in.

Hilda laughed. "Yes, the moment we've all been waiting for. Let's take a look at our CoreChart."

The room filled with pleasant chatter and then applause.

Andy smiled. He never tired of the energy he felt in a room full of aligned, engaged people. They had worked hard, and judging from the smiles on each person's face, they felt it was worth it. He stepped to the center of the room while the employees clapped for the Culture Team. He explained that turning core values into a valued culture meant going from simply having a core values poster on the wall to having core values embodied in each decision and strategy through Core People Processes—the hiring, unhiring, and evaluating protocols based on CoreVals.

"It's important to have a process to remove, or unhire, people who don't fit the culture or the team to preserve the harmony and greater good of the group." Andy reminded them that applying protocols evenly increased integrity and created trust among the team.

Leslie thought back to the meeting she had several weeks ago with Andy and Hilda when they ranked and rated the current team. Using the CoreScore as their objective tool for cultural fit, they'd determined that there were a few people who needed to be unhired. It was validating to see that the complainers, the eye rollers, and the baggage bringers were the ones who scored as poor cultural fits. This, of course, included Richard.

She used to dread that inevitable meeting with Richard, but when the time actually came, she was empowered to change the people in order to transform the culture. She had kept the meeting short and the conversation tied to culture.

"Richard," she had begun. "As you know, we're investing in Everco's culture. We know from the Culture Fulfillment process that when we're working with aligned employees who share the same values as the company, the work experience is more enjoyable and fulfilling for individuals. How do you feel you fit with Everco's cultural definitions?"

Leslie showed Richard their draft of CoreVals.

"What about We Only Live Once? Are you having fun here with the team?"

Richard smirked and shook his head. Leslie expected him to get defensive, but he didn't.

She considered the CoreVals again.

"Let's talk about Collaborative & Noble Service? Do you feel you are committed to Everco's cause? Do you enjoy serving not-for-profits? It seems you are often unhappy with the volume of sales and your commissions. Is that true?"

"Yes, it's true," Richard agreed. "That's why I keep trying to sell us to corporations with a lot of money." He flashed his wide smile.

"Well," Leslie retorted. "That's not a fit with who we are and where we're going." She referred to the next value, Go the Extra Mile. "One subtext for this value is pursuing the excitement of growth, yet I notice the same problems keep occurring in sales. We're not solving and improving. This makes me question if there's a fit between your strength and our value."

Richard held up his hand to stop her. "I see where this is going, and yes, I'd be better off elsewhere. In fact, I've started the job search. Frankly, I'm relieved to be talking about it."

"I see," Leslie said. "So should we agree that you're going to move on? Can we put a thirty-day time frame on that?"

"Yes, that's works," Richard replied. His shoulders relaxed as if a weight had been lifted.

Leslie asked him to use the upcoming month to introduce some of the sales team to his clients and reinforced that this did not need to affect their friendship.

After their meeting ended, Leslie wondered why she had ever been afraid of that conversation. She knew it was because she didn't have a tool like CoreScore. Once she had the tool and the CoreVals, she was able to step into that difficult conversation with Richard and the other poor fits for Everco's culture.

Andy's voice grew louder from the center of the room and interrupted her thoughts.

"Rest assured, team," he encouraged. "You will all have a chance to let us know how you feel about the culture here."

He told them that in order to keep the culture thriving, they would need to be intentional on a daily basis. They would develop a common language surrounding the values and talk about them daily. He explained that now that the values were established, they should feel empowered to Notice & Nominate and Catch & Correct.

"Prepare yourselves to observe when others are behaving in ways that serve Everco's culture. In those cases, we can give positive feedback and even nominate them for an award."

Andy discussed the nomination process and rewards as ways to ensure the values didn't just end up being empty words on the wall but were really thriving in the workplace.

"Another way to do that is to observe when others are straying from the values. Catch & Correct allows you to point out behaviors not in alignment with values. We want to be empowered to say something to an individual who is not behaving in alignment with a value in the same way we're confident to notice when someone is acting in alignment with the CoreVals."

He shared that they would soon begin to see posters going up around Everco.

"We want to make sure the work doesn't stop there, however. We want to continue living these values with our teammates, our clients, and our vendors. We want to use our newly defined values each day."

As Andy concluded the event, he thanked them for their time and left them with one final reminder. "As I hope you have learned, cultivating culture is not a job for leaders alone. It is done by champions like yourself. Most people work, but how many people love where they work and why they work? My goal was to help you unearth a truly valued culture where you are all valued and feel you are doing something meaningful. It's about creating environments of inclusion, connection, and authenticity. It's also about making each and every individual feel like they belong to something bigger than themselves. When we feel included, it creates community. I thank you for allowing me to share in Everco's community."

Andy relayed that he would see them again at the Check-in and Training in six weeks. In the meantime, he committed to continue working with the Culture Team and conducting Post Launch surveys to keep Everco's culture alive, thriving, and driving performance.

Chapter 8: Check-in and Training

HILDA SAT BEFORE THE entire team, some in-person and some joining virtually, to kick off Everco's first monthly all-company town hall meeting. In order to make their Core-Vals thrive and encourage the behaviors they wanted the team to emulate, Hilda began by telling a story about an employee selected for the CoreVal award that week. She and Leslie loved the process of sifting through the Notice & Nominate submissions. In fact, Hilda felt like it might be the new high-point in her professional life. Together, they had selected several winners, but in all honesty, it had been a difficult choice. The teams seemed to be enjoying the new core values awards and were enthusiastically nominating one another.

Hilda asked Nia to share her story of recognition.

"I'd be happy to," Nia responded. "Aarman is nothing short of amazing. He stepped up to solve a billing report problem and compile a list of clients to invoice. It was outside his area of experience and took up his evening. He always goes above and beyond what is necessary to get the job done. That's why I nominated him for being a "GEM" and Going the Extra Mile."

Next Hilda asked Deshawn to share his nomination story.

He retold the story of overhearing Mateo speaking with a client who was having trouble with a campaign.

"He dropped everything to help the client solve the issue, even though he could have passed her on to another team member. But that would not have been nearly as responsive for the client. Instead, he "DAREd" to Deliver a Remarkable Experience."

Hilda thanked him for sharing and asked for their final CoreVals nomination story from Erika.

Erika shared that when she was working on a project with Uri, they were experiencing a lot of pressure from the client to move up the deadline.

"He was so gracious in how he responded. He held firm to the deadline and explained to the client that creative teams needed time to move 'at the pace of peace.' I felt supported and safe to put my creative energies to good use without being pressured. That's why I nominated Uri for Collaborative & Noble Service.

Hilda explained that Aarman, Mateo, and Uri would get to choose prizes for behaving in concert with Everco's CoreVals. She thanked them all for their nominations and reminded them this was one way to keep the culture alive, thriving, and driving performance.

In the four weeks since Everco's launch, the culture already felt different. Leslie had received positive feedback about the Launch Event and already recognized that individuals were more accountable and teams were more aligned. She knew much of that was because the right people were being hired and retained—thanks to Hilda's use of CoreScore and their newly founded behavior-based interview questions.

Leslie also understood that many of these measurables were not only informed by who they did hire, but also the poor cultural fits who were respectfully unhired. Though those six conversations, the first involving Richard, were difficult, Leslie let the core values guide her. She found the exchanges went much more smoothly, and she remained confident during each one.

Now, as Leslie addressed her employees at their first town hall, she acknowledged the recent unhires. She reassured them the company was doing well and there was nothing to worry about. Rather than being alarmed by the recent unhires, most people agreed with them. During Culture Fulfillment, it became clear that some people were not strong fits, and that they were dragging the rest of Everco down. They were now working with like-minded people without the sufferance of detractors.

Emboldened by her conversation with Richard and others, Leslie had also used CoreVals to navigate difficult conversations that she previously might have avoided. Just last week when an account manager was complaining about the lack of good leads from marketing, she'd walked him over to the CoreVals poster and reminded him that at Everco, they valued GEM or Going the Extra Mile. This meant that it was in their DNA to get creative and find ways to grow. She also referenced their CANS value of Collaboration & Noble Service that meant she needed him to commit, not complain, and realize that he was working with good people in marketing who might need extra support.

She recognized that she was essentially using the CoreVals to hold him accountable. She was amazed that she had not tapped this obvious and easy technique years ago, but she was grateful to have it now.

Leslie covered the rest of the town hall agenda by updating the team on the "high points and happenings" of the company over the prior month as well as highlighting what was coming up in the next month.

As she concluded the townhall meeting, she reminded her teams that Andy would be returning soon to gauge how well the newly defined cultural definitions were resonating with them. Though Leslie was interested to see the results from Andy's assessment, she was really looking forward to the training session to learn more ways to keep their CoreVals thriving and driving Everco's performance.

$$***$$

Six weeks after the Launch Event, Leslie and the rest of the Culture Team came together for a Check-In and Training. Andy had spent the week prior conducting interviews of selected employees and members of the Culture Team. He updated the team on his findings, and then they had a picnic lunch under the Blue Spruce outside the office.

It was a great opportunity to connect. Crissy even led them through a grounding meditation she often used at Everco's informal "Spruce Your Blues" sessions. Afterwards, Fred boasted about the fish he and his grandson had caught that weekend, and Crissy gushed about the new baby goats she and her partner Agatha were raising. Hilda updated them on the progress of her home renovation, and Sid announced that he had finally begun the triathlon training he had wanted to do for a decade.

Now, back in the office, they turned their focus to Culture Fulfillment. Andy reminded them that the real work of culture began after the poster was posted.

"Great cultures drive great performance. As you have seen from your own experience, in great cultures, everyone is accountable and pulling together. Teams make decisions the same way that leadership would, and difficult conversations that promote healthy, safe relationships are embraced, not avoided. Our goal at this Check-In and Training is to ensure we are using core values every day."

Andy explained that one way to measure whether their CoreVal work was resonating with teams and leaders was through the company-wide Post Launch Surveys he and Hilda had initiated last week. He said that the survey would help them determine how much things had improved since Everco's recent investment in its cultural definition. He shared a sample of the questions and some of the results he wanted to highlight.

Andy started by displaying before and after scores for culture.

"Looking at these results, it's clear that even though we thought we had a pretty good culture before we started, we still had a dramatic improvement in scoring. This certainly

Post Launch Survey

1. Prior to our recent culture launch, what score would you give the company for having an effective approach to sustaining culture? 1-10

2. Please explain your answer.

3. Today, post launch, what score would you give the company for having an effective approach to sustaining culture? 1-10

4. Please explain your answer.

5. Have you noticed our leaders affirming the culture in meetings and on an ad hoc basis? Yes or No

6. Have you noticed employees affirming the culture in meetings and on an ad hoc basis? Yes or No

7. Are the company's core values more memorable and referable now? Yes or No

8. Have the posters and other collateral improved the memorability of the core values? Yes or No

9. Have you noticed whether leaders hire and unhire in line with culture? Yes or No

10. Please explain your answer.
11. Overall, do you feel better about working in the company? Yes or No.
12. Please explain your answer.
13. How well is the core values Notice & Nominate program working? 1-10
14. Please explain your answer
15. Do you love where you work, who you work with, and why you work? 1-10
16. Has being more aware of the company's Core Purpose—or why—increased the fulfillment you feel from your work? 1-10

proves that culture is measurable and that significant Returns on Culture are possible."

When he showed the results for Everco's effective approach to sustaining culture, he clapped.

"Congrats, Leadership and Culture Team. These results show that the confidence in your ability to manage an effective

Employee NPS® Scores

Before

What score would you give the company for having a great culture?

NPS® Score   40

During

What score would you give the company for having a great culture?

NPS® Score   70

approach to sustaining culture has gone from about fifty percent scoring eight and above to more than ninety-five percent scoring eight and above! You should all feel incredibly proud."

"In other good news, let's consider the next highlight. With seventy-six of the respondents scoring the company at

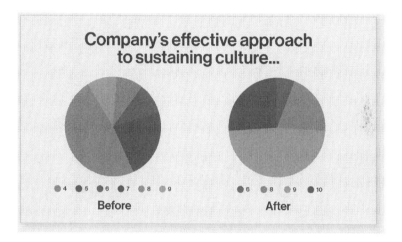

nine and above, we can be confident that our team is pretty content here on a high bar question of loving where they work, who they work with, and why they work. I'm sure you agree this is a very gratifying response indeed."

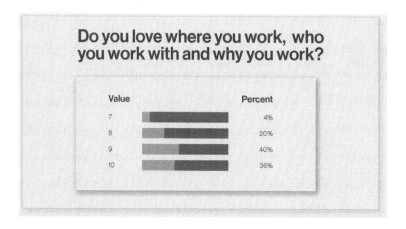

"As you know," Andy continued. "I had the pleasure of speaking with some of you and a small group of employees for our Post Launch Employee Interviews. This allowed us to gather more feedback about what is and is not working with our culture."

Andy shared a sample of the questions he posed.

What do you think of the Cultural Definition?

    - Values and descriptive behaviors?

    - CorePurpose?

    - The Image?

What did you think of the Launch Event?

    - Like

    - Improvements?

What do you think of the Notice & Nominate scheme?

Have you heard people mention them?

    - Leaders

    - Colleagues?

How confident are you that we will maintain this culture going forward?

Have you heard about CoreScore yet from leaders?

Can you remember the core values?

Anything else I should have asked?

"Now, let's take a look at some of those results," Andy said.

He gave them a few minutes to read through before adding, "These are exactly the kind of qualitative answers we would hope for and further illustrate not only the value of investing in our culture but the obvious net effect that we've had."

What do you think of the Cultural Definition?

Employee #1: Well thought out. Gave me chills. Made a lot of sense. Visuals make it more real. Gives purpose to the words. Remembers each of the images that go with the values.

Employee #2: Liked values before. Liked taking time to be intentional. Felt worthwhile. Incorporating image was huge. Likes serving with a core purpose. We are a money making business and actively serving.

Employee #3: Feels like ourselves from five years ago. Liked having an external point of view to push to completion. We are not done, but we are on the right trajectory. New voices are involved. Great experience.

Next, Andy wanted to discuss the Notice & Nominate scheme, which was a way to encourage behaviors that served Everco's culture. He shared that they had received a total of forty-five nominations since its inception: fifteen for Collaborative & Noble Service, fourteen for We Only Live Once, ten for Deliver a Remarkable Experience, and six for Go the Extra Mile. He also reported that after the initial flurry of nominations, Hilda had seen a decrease in nominations in the last couple of weeks. He also said that several employees had mentioned during their interviews that they weren't recognizing people because they were unsure their nomination was written well enough. Together the team discussed how they might improve the scheme.

Hilda took notes to capture their answers.

How might Everco improve our Notice & Nominate scheme?

Offer periodic reminders

It's never too big or too small to recognize

Write about any story - we will not judge

Just get it in, it doesn't need to be perfect

Andy encouraged Leslie to speak to the employees and assure them that Notice & Nominate wasn't about perfect writing but rather about letting Everco know when something great happened. Leslie agreed to send out a reminder to the employees before next month's townhall to submit the CoreVal nominations. The team recognized this was an important initiative to continue.

For the next portion of the training, Andy wanted to discuss another important tool that practiced drawing on the CoreVals to discourage behaviors that didn't serve Everco's culture—Catch & Correct.

Andy explained some best practices to adhere to when using Catch & Correct, like staying within the intent of the CoreVals and correcting with candor but without hurting feelings.

"In order for this scheme to be effective," he explained. "We must all remain committed to giving and receiving feedback. I also recommend doing the correction in the moment, when appropriate."

Andy said that in order for Catch & Correct to work, there must be a prerequisite of trust. "That's why we don't launch into this practice right away but let the organization be with their new culture using the easier Notice & Nominate for a few weeks before teaching Catch & Correct." He said the leaders and employees must encourage each other and show one another grace as they observe others stepping into the tactic.

"You can encourage people to have difficult conversations—even if done imperfectly. Over time, everyone will become skilled at the tactic, and the organization will be the stronger for it and gain further competitive advantage and team performance.

"There are always opportunities to applaud initiative," Andy reminded them. "Take those any time you can."

Andy now felt it was time to turn from teaching to experiential learning, which he knew to be more powerful. He asked the Culture Team to break into four groups, one per value. Once the team was in groups, Andy asked that they discuss behaviors they had observed or might imagine happening that didn't fit the value.

"From the situations that your group comes up with," Andy said. "Choose two and ask yourselves what the Catch & Correct dialog might sound like. I'd like for you to rehearse it and then role play for everyone. The more we can practice these conversations, the more at ease we are with them in real-life situations."

When each team was finished, they role played the difficult conversations. This allowed the group to develop a language that would help them interact and stay aligned with values.

For the final portion of the training, Andy turned it over to Hilda. As she briefly left the room to gather her supplies, a videographer joined them and set up his equipment. They would document the next portion of the training to use with new employees. The footage he recorded earlier of employees talking about CoreVals would also become part of their culture video that would document their Culture Fulfillment journey.

Hilda asked the team to make a pathway through the room by clearing the tables and chairs and organized the teams in their groups according to the flow of the client journey.

"One of our objectives today," Hilda began, "is to discover—through an experiential process—exactly what our clients are feeling and what values we bring to their experiences at each stage of the process and to consider our departmental handoffs, from the clients' viewpoint. I really want us to put ourselves in their shoes, make sure that they are experiencing the values that we espouse, and reinforce the learning around our CoreWorkflow at the same time. Let's step through it."

The team plotted out the client's journey and had Sid move through the room from team to team with everyone contributing to the nuances, touch-points, and hand-offs. When the customer journey was complete, Hilda asked everyone to stay in their places except for Sid, who she asked to join her back at the start of the trail. "I want us to repeat this process," Hilda said. "But this time, I want us to say what the customer feels at each stage and what values we are bringing to that portion of the journey."

When they were finished, Hilda asked that they repeat the process a third time, but this time consider what support groups might be required for each portion of the journey. Together, they discussed how Marketing, Software, HR, and Finance teams supported the front line teams throughout the process.

When they had completed the exercise, Andy congratulated them.

"Hilda, this is a really experiential way to learn what Everco's clients are feeling and how the CoreVals fit with the work we do every day."

As the Check-In and Training concluded, there was a playful, connected energy in the room. They played their newly chosen theme song as Hilda handed out Everco backpacks that included puzzles, hats, compasses, and even shirts that had Everco's CorePurpose printed on the back. Hilda explained that all employees would receive the same gifts.

Some of the Culture Team proudly put their shirts on over their clothes. Seeing the words emblazoned on the back put an exclamation point on the day. Everyone in the room—and everyone in Everco—now knew what the company was about, where they fit, and how best to operate.

While the Culture Team admired their swag, Andy said, "The next step in Culture Fulfillment is to let you all continue to cultivate your culture. I will return in 3 months for a Prove & Improve event. Thank you all so much for your effort and collaboration. I am excited to see how your culture thrives in the next several months. In the meantime, I will stay in touch with Hilda to continue supporting Everco's Culture Fulfillment."

Chapter 9: Prove & Improve

TWO MONTHS HAD PASSED since the Post Launch Check-In and Training. Since that time, the morale of the teams remained high, but for Hilda, some things felt like they were slipping. Although she had continued to use the CoreScore and behavior-based interview questions for hiring, she felt like new employees were not getting the values-based training they needed. She discussed this with Andy during lunch, and together they drafted a plan to build in cultural measurements that would ensure a values-centric training approach for new hires.

Add employees' CoreScores to their files," he encouraged. "And discuss core values during evaluative meetings. Create one or more baseline questions about culture to ask every employee at evaluation time. Adding cultural markers to your evaluation structure won't cost Everco more, and it will give you one additional way to measure culture."

Andy was Hilda's trusted partner, and once again, his advice would serve her and Everco well. In fact, during last week's surveys and this morning's interviews, he had uncovered even more insights into how Everco could continue to sustain a valued culture. Though Andy had shared his findings with her already, she was eager for the rest of the Culture Team to learn the results.

Now, as she waited for the team to assemble for their Prove & Improve cycle, she noticed how different the feeling was at Everco. Six months ago, there was little conversation while waiting for meetings to start. People usually had their heads down, staring at their phones—or in Fred's case, shuffling his papers. Today, people seemed genuinely excited to have the free time to be together and check in with each other. The conversations were going deeper, and people were sharing more of who they were—not just about their current Everco tasks, but about their lives and families, their passions, their hopes.

As they waited, Sid was excitedly telling Fred about his improved running time. He had been asking Fred, who had undergone heart surgery several years ago, to join him on a daily walk. After several weeks of Fred refusing, Sid had brought in a handmade fly fishing lure that his uncle had made. Fred marveled at the detail and craftsmanship.

"It can be yours," Sid told him. "If you walk with me today."

"Son, are you bribing me?" Fred asked.

"It's only a bribe if it works," Sid laughed.

"Has anyone ever told you that your persistence is irksome?" Fred asked with a slight smile.

"All the time," Sid replied.

That same day, Hilda spotted the two out the window walking slowly down the block. Every day since then, the pair walked. In fact, other members of Everco joined in, and before long, employees had self-organized a lunch activity that included a grounding meditation under the Blue Spruce, stretching exercises, and walking.

As Hilda watched people conversing before the meeting, she couldn't be sure if it was the exercise, mountain air, or social connection, but the Culture Team looked livelier than ever. She felt grateful to be working at a place she loved with people she genuinely liked and doing work that she knew made a difference.

As Andy started the meeting, he reviewed what he and Hilda had discussed would enhance the training of new hires. He reminded them that one of their greatest tools was the video they had filmed during the Check-In and Training.

"What better way to remind the new hires what Everco cares about, not only the client's service journey through the organization, but their emotional journey as well? Use the townhalls and daily huddles to continue talking about Core-Vals. We want them in the hearts and minds of all. And the best way to do that is by talking about them and living them ourselves."

"As you know," Andy continued. "I spent the morning interviewing employees and leaders about how our cultural definitions are resonating with them. I'd like to review those findings and identify highlights," Andy said. "Overall, it seems that our culture is steadily becoming real in the hearts and minds of its people." Andy displayed Everco's NPS® score from before Culture Fulfillment and after.

Employee NPS® Scores

Before

What score would you give the company for having a great culture?

NPS® Score   40

During

What score would you give the company for having a great culture?

NPS® Score   70

After

What score would you give the company for having a great culture?

NPS® Score   90

"This gives us a better understanding of why we call this Prove & Improve," Andy explained. "Using quantitative data, we can prove that Everco's culture is more valued and valuable than it was when we started. Our goal now is to keep it going. We want to continue improving the lives of our people, clients, and vendors."

He clarified that though this was positive news, anonymous surveys wouldn't help identify areas for improvements like interviews would. It was for that reason that Andy had spent the morning interviewing leaders and employees in an effort to delve deeper into how the cultural definitions were resonating. Andy displayed the questions he had asked during those conversations.

Prove & Improve Interview Questions

What did you think of the Check-In and Training Event?

What do you think of the Notice & Nominate scheme?

What do you think of the Catch & Correct scheme? Do people find it easier to step into difficult conversations and use the Catch & Correct dialogues we practiced?

Have you heard people mention them?

How confident are you that we will maintain this culture going forward?

Have you heard about CoreScore yet from leaders?

Can you remember the core values?

Since we launched, what sustained changes have you noticed?

Are we working with more aligned clients?

Do we have a more cohesive group working together more

effectively? Can you tell me an example or story about cohesive teams?

Are the leaders demonstrating a culture first style of leadership?

On a scale of 1-10, what score would you give Everco for having a great culture? Ok, what would make it a 10?

Anything else I should have asked?

Next, Andy shared the first issue unearthed from the interviews:

Issue #1: "We're doing a great job with culture, but I don't see leaders doing anything with it. They're too busy to do the Nomination scheme.

Andy explained that leaders had to model the behaviors they wanted to see. "We have to show people what we're looking for. We have to do what we're asking them to do." He acknowledged this sounded easier than it was, but he also knew that Everco's Culture Team was eager and enthusiastic about continuing to cultivate a valued culture.

Issue #2: "Even the leaders don't remember the values. In fact, there aren't even posters up in some departments yet."

The team agreed that this was an oversight on their part. They put the effort into the iterative work and in ordering and distributing swag, but they hadn't followed through with all of the printing.

"Don't underestimate the power of being able to point to the values and make them a part of your conversations," Andy urged. "When you need to step into difficult conversations, walk people over to the CoreChart. Point to the values. Remind employees why you are all here. Let the CoreChart be the visual guide to walk you through values-based conversations."

Issue #3: "I thought we're supposed to be leading a culture, not just a company, but I haven't seen anyone talking to clients and vendors about values. There is one client who wears me down and no one has stepped in to correct them or shown me how to extend our culture to them. "

"This is great feedback," Andy said. "This is an opportunity to remember that values need to be communicated outside Everco and should be used to screen and onboard vendors as well as clients."

As Andy explained, one of Everco's values was Deliver a Remarkable Experience, but that didn't mean the team should bend over backwards for a lousy client who drained them. He encouraged them that if the client wasn't adhering to the value, and didn't respond to feedback, unhiring was an option that could be good for everybody.

"Let's try a helpful test," Andy said. He reminded them of the CoreScore they were already using to assess current and new hires. "Using the same method, score clients against each value. If they are deemed a poor cultural fit, then we could unhire them for the health of the team and the company. Otherwise, both are being dragged down."

The team loved how easy and objective this was. They all agreed that they would use the CoreScore on all of their current clients and vendors, and it would certainly be explained to any potential new ones.

Andy reminded them to lean heavily on all the measurements they had used for culture, including quantitative surveys, overall CoreScore, and team CoreScores.

"When you initiated Culture Fulfillment, your natural curiosity about building culture was probably offset by what you would have to invest."

"Sounds familiar," Crissy muttered and smiled at Fred.

"It's true," Fred admitted. "It's literally my job to ask how much money—not to mention time and effort—this process would take. I'm the first to admit that I was skeptical. But I also admit that early on, I overlooked some exponential dividends."

"Fred, I love your honesty," Andy offered. "And this conversation naturally leads us to the final portion of Prove & Improve. I'd like for us to calculate Everco's Return on Culture. What has been the cost, and what is the ROC? What has implementing these 9 Deeds in Everco cost you?"

"Get your popcorn, Fred," Sid called. "It's the moment you've been waiting for!"

The team, along with Fred, laughed freely.

"Fred, would you like to walk us through the numbers?"

"It's always a pleasure to talk numbers," Fred answered.

Andy displayed the equation he had shared with them before, but this time—with Fred's help—he had plugged in the relevant numbers. Fred explained that most of the cost of Culture Fulfillment was in time and other internal resources that Everco was already carrying. Other costs included printing and promotional products, like the swag they'd distributed after the Launch Event.

"Generally speaking," Fred said. "It's nothing complicated. Let's break it down. We're a ten million dollar company and we're operating pretty close to breakeven. My forecast predicts that we will be at twenty percent profitability next quarter, thanks to working with better clients, having a more cohesive team, and our improved efficiency. But let's do the calculation based on our gains last quarter. We achieved a ten percent uptick in profit, which I can attribute to our improved culture making the numerator $100,000. Everco spent roughly ten hours per week, over the nine weeks we walked through the 9 Deeds, at an internal cost of fifty dollars per hour. Then, the team time cost is approximately $4,500. Another $5,500 was spent on printing, giveaways, T-shirts, and some event costs, for a total numerator cost of $10,000. This results in a ten times return on investment to date and doesn't begin to account for what we will do over a twelve month period or going forward."

"Many companies I have worked with," Andy added, "would easily accept that they have netted a ten times return or more. And some would credit the project with yielding a much higher profit lift than ten percent."

The team agreed that investing in Everco's culture had been worth it. Their revenues were up, their profits were up, and their teams were more focused, engaged, and happy.

"Data like this gives us a richer picture of the complex workplace dynamic that is culture. Identifying measurable

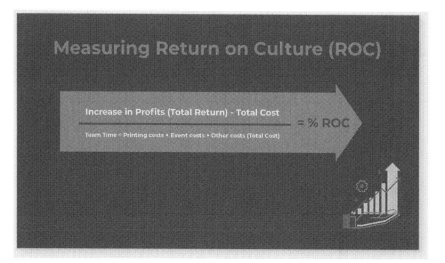

results will give direction on how to proceed, based on what is working."

Andy said the surveys, interviews, and ROC showed them how culture drove Everco's business. And when everything moved in synchronicity, they would notice improvements in team and company performance. If the culture was strong, people would stay in their jobs and perform them well. That meant less money would be spent on recruitment and severance, and potentially more money would be coming in if the market was responsive. This was yet another reason why gathering data on the condition of Everco's culture was worthwhile. Andy reminded them that he would continue to return to conduct quarterly Prove & Improve training to help them keep the culture alive, thriving, and driving performance.

"In closing, remember that few elements of doing business are more important than a culture that includes top people performing to their full potential in a tight team that is meeting or exceeding its goals—and having fun doing it!"

Sid said they had that part covered, and the team agreed they were all having fun. And they were. You could tell from their faces and from the genuine regard for one another. They understood that not only had Culture Fulfillment created an atmosphere that made them want to show up to work every day, but it had a ripple effect on their individual lives that made them happier, more balanced, and more fulfilled. Each of them now understood how Everco's culture was their greatest business asset.

Chapter 10: Onward and Upward

IT HAD BEEN ALMOST a year since Leslie called Andy and asked for his help at Everco. At the time, she hadn't even known what was lacking in her company, but with Andy's help, she now realized it was an underdeveloped and atrophied culture that was causing so many obstacles for her employees and teams.

Now, as the team gathered for their final Check-In, Leslie felt it was a bittersweet moment. She was certainly proud of the work the Culture Team and employees had invested into fulfilling their culture and maintaining it, but she also felt wistful about not having Andy's regular training and teaching for much longer. He had assured her he would always be a phone call away if they wanted to refresh their training or needed his support, but for now, he was confident they could sustain their valued culture.

As the rest of the Culture Team joined Leslie in the conference room, there was a playful energy surrounding them. Leslie assumed that some of that was because they were reviving their picnics, which would take place after today's training. The event staff, led by Sid, had taken the picnic planning very seriously and assured the employees it would be the best one yet.

Andy asked how the team was feeling and the first word Leslie thought of was pride. She had never before enjoyed the pure pride that came from building something from the ground up—not just Everco itself but also its valued culture.

She thought back to watching her mom operate a not-for-profit, and she wondered if her mother had ever been able to feel what Leslie now felt. She knew from her experience with the Entrepreneurs' Organization that many leaders got so tied up in the stresses of owning a business that there was little room for feelings like pride. She was grateful for the experience that allowed her this feeling. She understood there was no way to measure the personal benefits that a valued culture had on her and her family.

In the last several weeks, Leslie had started taking Wednesday mornings for herself. On those days, she went into work late so that she could spend extra time with her son before school. Then, she would meditate and take a long hike before heading to work. A year ago, taking the time to invest in her mental and spiritual health seemed impossible. What a difference a year made!

In fact, she and her family were even embarking on a two-week vacation the next day. It was the first real vacation Leslie had taken since starting Everco. Though she technically could have stepped away before, she hadn't been sure her teams could have handled things. Now, with her teams working in concert and able to make decisions in her absence, she felt confident that things would continue smoothly. She now understood that in a great culture, there wasn't a need to rely solely on one person because people were accountable in new ways, thanks to values and culture-first leadership.

As Andy kicked off the final Check-In, he reminded the team how far they had come and how much he appreciated their insights and collaboration.

"Today is a day to celebrate the valued culture that we have brought alive, made thrive, and used to drive Everco's performance."

It was true that the company's performance had benefited. Revenues and profits were up. Teams were working well and were more focused, in part because their clients were a better fit with their culture, and their projects suited their capabilities. Thanks to their CoreWorkflow, they were working more efficiently with better communication between departments and were getting things right the first time rather than reworking them. People were enjoying working together and were even meeting up outside of work. More employees were also volunteering their time for pro bono work. Since they had revamped their hiring practices, they were adding more people who were good fits for the culture. Everco had even welcomed a new Chief Revenue Officer to the team—Vijay—who was aligned with their values and was already finding clients that were good cultural fits. He was bringing in work the team was good at and even asked for reasonable delivery dates before he committed to clients. In response, their profits were growing, and their teams were thriving.

Andy reminded them that when things were going well, it was tempting to get complacent. "At this stage of core value maintenance," he warned, "breakdown can occur—after the focus groups and surveys and system implementations, when passion for culture cools. If you focus on applying processes consistently and persistently, the culture continues on a positive trend."

Andy said the purpose of today's Check-In was to honor the work they had done and offer him any feedback they might have. He wanted to start their time together the same way they always had—with a centering exercise. He led them through a meditation to help them feel present and connected. Then, he asked them to take a few moments to think about the last year and notice what dysfunction they had purged, reduced, or avoided during their Culture Fulfillment work.

The team was silent as each person took stock of their own experience. After a couple of minutes, Andy asked them each to share one thing that came up for them.

Leslie answered that she no longer avoided difficult conversations. Hilda said she was pleased to be able to unhire negative employees. Sid and Crissy both agreed that they were happy to be aligned with clients and vendors who shared their values and how much easier the work felt as a result. Fred offered that he was most pleased that there was a stronger commitment to people doing what they said they would do and what a difference that had made.

The entire team then brainstormed several other issues they were happy to leave behind, like fear of conflict, lack of trust, and other antisocial behaviors. Andy noted all their answers on the whiteboard.

What dysfunctional business aspects have we reduced or purged?

- negative employees
- difficult conversation avoidance
- fear of conflict
- lack of trust
- avoidance of accountability
- disregard for team objectives
- harassment or other anti-social behaviors

Next, Andy asked them to think of something they appreciated about Everco's culture today versus in the past. After several quiet minutes of contemplation, the team was eager to offer their answers.

Crissy said she was surprised at how much having a Core-Purpose had positively impacted her attitude at work.

"Of course, it has helped to have a more balanced life," she added. "I appreciate that my teammates value the same work/life balance that I do—not only value it, but encourage and support it!"

Last month, Crissy had been promoted to Head of Design. Rather than avoid leadership roles as she had in the past, she embraced Everco's new culture-first leadership and led the design team while working from home a couple days a week. This allowed her to continue her work at Everco while pursuing the homesteading passion that brought her and her family such fulfillment.

It was true that Everco had started to prioritize their employees' mental, physical, and emotional health in new ways. Being present was lauded, and rushing to tackle task after task was discouraged. Leaders encouraged this mindset by stopping and checking in with teams to affirm values and goals. Moving "at the pace of peace" had become company lingo and a reminder they shared readily. Most employees would agree that practicing this perspective at work had impacted their home lives as well. To this end, Everco had invited employees to restructure their time. Most employees were now working fewer hours, yet their productivity had improved. Andy noted this was one benefit of having a Core-Purpose.

"When teams are all working in concert toward a common goal," Andy said. "There is more engagement with the work and therefore an increased efficiency. I am happy that you all are feeling that."

Hilda shared that her work experience had improved because she had a language for Catch & Correct.

"It helps that I know—and everyone knows—the value-based expectations and the language to address deviant behaviors. It feels like there is less pressure on the leadership now." She said the safer she felt at Everco, the more empowered she became to hire and unhire according to values. She understood that she wasn't the only one feeling this way. It felt like a new Everco where everyone was empowered to use CoreVals. Just last week, she'd used the power of their declared values to correct an employee's behavior when Sora criticized another employee in her presence. Her response was direct and value-based.

"Sora, one of our values includes being kind, and you just disparaged a teammate," Hilda said.

Sora thought for a moment before saying, "You're right, Hilda. I'm sorry. I'll try not to do that again."

There was no argument, and it was an opportunity to model the values-based lesson for anyone else around.

"And when we need to have those conversations," Leslie added. "We don't avoid them and let the employees and teams fester with resentment. That has been a game-changer."

As the Culture Team continued to share the positive attributes that had improved or increased, Andy noted them on the whiteboard.

**What positive attributes have improved
or increased since establishing a valued culture?**
- purpose
- language for Catch & Correct
- mental, physical, and spiritual health of all
- morale
- teamwork
- motivation
- commitment
- goal achievement
- performance
- shifted culture from chaos to order
- great clients aligned with values

Andy encouraged the team to keep the two lists they had generated handy as a means to prevent regression. "When you fear the culture is slipping or teams seem complacent, simply keep in mind the dysfunctional aspects of business that good culture has helped you avoid, reduce, or purge and the functional aspects it has helped you increase or improve."

Andy was confident in Everco's culture-first leadership and congratulated them on graduating from his tutelage.

"I am confident that Hilda and Everco's new Chief Culture Officer can competently sustain their culture-first leadership."

Here Andy paused, and the team applauded Sid, who had just last month stepped into a new role at Everco as CCO. His responsibility would be to cultivate culture in their current office and the new office they would open within the year. He also helped Hilda with onboarding, training and interviewing, supported the sales teams with new clients, and planned events that would help keep their culture alive. Today's picnic was his first event, and he had assured them that it would be memorable.

"Hilda and Sid will have access to The Culture Fix Academy," Andy said, bringing their meeting to a close. "This will provide access to the same full suite of tools—from the methodologies to the strategies, from surveys to case studies, from sample scripts to instructional videos—we used during the iterative process of turning Everco's core values into a valued culture."

He encouraged them to reach out at any time if he could be of service.

"But for now," he explained. "It's onward and upward for Everco, and we have a picnic celebration to attend."

***

The team was in high spirits as they assembled with the rest of Everco's employees in the park near their building. For some of the remote workers, this was the first time they were meeting face-to-face. Most employees wore their shirts emblazoned with Everco's CorePurpose, and Sid distributed more shirts to the friends and family who joined the celebration.

Once everyone had gathered, Sid took to the small stage and thanked them for coming. He said this event, beloved in the past, was now reinstated as an annual event.

When an employee yelled, "Can we make it monthly?" the crowd laughed and cheered.

"I'll work on that," Sid responded, smiling broadly. "But for now, let's eat!"

As people mingled around the picnic tables, it was hard to tell this was a work event, considering the laughter and fun that surrounded them. Once everyone had eaten, Sid rolled out the speakers and a karaoke machine. The employees clapped as Fred took the stage.

"As you all know, today is my last day at Everco." The crowd quickly became more somber. "It's not a sad day for me because I know I'm the old guard, and it's time to pass the torch. Everco is in good hands."

He smiled at Leslie, and she raised her glass to him.

"And, besides," he continued. "I'm tired of looking at spreadsheets all day. I want to spend my days on the water fishing and looking into the eyes of my big catch."

The crowd applauded again.

"Now, you old timers like me remember that karaoke used to be an integral part of Everco's picnics. I'm happy to see that Sid will be carrying on the tradition. But, before I go, let this old dog perform one last trick. Hit it, Sid."

Music filled the lot, and Fred performed a dramatic rendition of Conway Twitty's Hello Darling. When he stepped into the crowd to serenade his wife, Doris, the crowd went wild. After the song, Fred dipped Doris and planted a kiss on her. She blushed and laughed as the Everco team lined up to hug Fred and wish him luck on his retirement.

As Vijay took the mic to sing a lively Bohemian Rhapsody, Andy scanned the celebration. He noticed smiles everywhere. He spotted Leslie standing close to Fred and wiping her eyes. He understood it would be hard for Leslie to see Fred go. They had known each other for decades, but he knew Leslie was the kind of leader who could withstand disruptions like this. He also knew that Hilda, who was playing with some of the children, would find a replacement for Fred that would strengthen the team.

He felt the familiar feeling return to his gut that told him it was time to move on. There would be other leaders, other teams, other cultures that he could support and move to action.

He was honored to have actuated the dramatic change that had taken place at Everco this year. He still remembered walking in to Everco that first day, calm and confident, to find an environment that was anything but.

In that time, the company had changed, and the people changed all at the pace of peace. Their Culture Fulfillment wasn't forced. Rather, it was allowed to unfold in a natural, organic way. He was assured this group would sustain a culture so that people loved where they work and who they worked with and would continue to work for their CorePurpose and toward their CorePurpose.

Andy's phone rang. He answered and heard a frantic voice.

"Hi, Andy, I was recently talking to my friend Leslie from the Entrepreneurs' Organizations about some issues I'm having in my company. She suggested I give you a call. I need some support, but I don't know what kind. Can you help?"

Andy smiled. "Let me tell you about the Gift of Culture."

Conclusion

Begins and Ends with Culture

The real work of culture begins once Culture Fulfillment is complete. As Leslie and the rest of Everco's team learned, Culture Fulfillment is an ongoing investment in the people within an organization. As fun and rewarding as it is to design and display a gorgeous CoreChart that makes values more memorable and referable, the important work is in sustaining the culture and constantly bringing energy to it.

Why invest in culture in the first place? To create environments where people thrive so they can be the best they can be, and so employees love where they work, who they work with, and why they do the work.

Investing in culture isn't just about the corporate benefits, which are many, but also the human rewards. We know that humans have physiological needs like food and water, but we also need security, belonging, and feelings of achievement. In fact, many psychologists posit that humans are unable to achieve their full potential until these basic and psychological requirements are met. By investing in culture, leaders are able to meet the needs of their employees in new ways, allowing their teams to work using their full potential.

In my work with companies and organizations, I've seen how a great work culture sounds ideal, but there is something better. A company with a valued work culture motivates and empowers employees. It addresses the importance of why they do what they do, not just what they do.

Everco itself went from being unprofitable, chaotic, and burdened by unfit clients to being organized, efficient, noble, and empowered by aligned clients. The transformation from "great" to valued culture elevated Everco from a marketing company for non-profits to a company that exists to do good for those who do good, so more good gets done for the world.

And its people changed as a result. Leslie, once empowered by the process, stepped into her leadership role with the same ease she stepped into difficult conversations. Hilda had a similar experience and was able to embrace her role at Everco with her full potential. Fred, Sid, and Crissy also exemplified how feeling safe, seen, and significant at work can validate a person in ways that extend into their personal and family lives. In short, once Everco defined its purpose, it freed all employees to bring their whole selves, pursue the joy of growth and creativity, and have fun doing it!

Whether in the pages of this book or in the lives of my clients' employees, I've learned that once people feel aligned and competent, they can live their best lives. Though Everco is a fictional organization, its Culture Fulfillment is based on the actual transformations I have observed in my clients' companies. Everco doesn't represent every outcome, but it does represent the desired outcome and the highly likely one. How do I know? Because despite culture's ephemerality, it can be measured. One of the ways we do this is by asking employees the same question at the start and end of Culture Fulfillment: "What score would you give the company for having a great culture?" It is not uncommon to achieve thirty-five to fifty percent or more improvement in the NPS® score in just four months with this proven process. We also use the CoreScore—a numeric measurement that indicates the degree to which employees and teams work in concert with CoreVals—to measure improvements. As you read in these chapters, we also conduct a Post Launch Survey to measure employees' belief in the company's ability to lead a great culture going forward. We often see these numbers increase significantly, indicating that having a valued culture also enhances people's faith in the company.

When I began fulfilling culture in my own companies decades ago, I quickly learned that investing in my people was an investment in much more. This is when I learned how powerful the Gift of Culture is to environments, people, and teams. I began helping others invest in their culture, and as the need became greater than my time allowed, I created The Culture Fix Academy to enable people—whether in their own companies or in others' companies—to move others to action. With TCF Academy, Actuators and Self-Actuators can bring a valued culture alive so that it thrives and can be used to drive performance. It not only gives people a system for actuating a great culture, it also gives them a method for sustaining it once it has been fulfilled.

At TCF Academy, we train Actuators and Self-Actuators how to take organizations from simply having core values to truly having a valued culture. This is achieved when employees, associates, and stakeholders feel valued and believe they are making meaningful contributions every day. We don't dream it up or stamp our idea of culture on an organization. We fulfill the best of what exists within. We don't just show up, workshop a team and disappear. We invest over the course of months and care as much as the people do. We don't make it up as we go along. We deliver the proven 9 Deeds in 90 Days—just as Andy did at Everco.

Strategy is to thought as culture is to feeling. If you only have the former, you're missing what it is to be human and overlooking opportunities to lead people and experience more engagement. Global research has repeatedly shown that the majority of employees feel disengaged from the work they do. This is nothing less than a malaise, a real illness that is affecting workplaces around the world. At The Culture Fix Academy, we are committed to flipping that ratio. We are on a mission to usher in a decade of conscious leadership to cure the malaise of employee disengagement. We want employees to feel fulfilled, loyal, and engaged so that they don't work to live but rather have one fulfilling life.

After reading this book, it is my hope that a leader understands they are not just the leader of a company; they are the leader of a culture—a much more grandiose and fulfilling leadership role with a greater mission and purpose. There is no nobler journey that a CEO or entrepreneur can embark upon than enhancing their organizational culture. It requires the lowest investment, yields the highest return, and is fun and rewarding for everyone involved. Many companies have core values on the wall but have not created a valued culture where people thrive and are the best that they can be. When you lead a team with your core values as a compass, you are contributing to a new style of leadership that is less about strength and assertiveness, and more about inclusion, connection, and authenticity.

When an individual feels included, it creates community. Outside of all of the quantifiable returns we've witnessed from Everco's Culture Fulfillment, imagine the benefits of creating this sense of community for the people on a team. Having seen the transformations that a valued culture can bring to workplaces and organizations, many people implement the same changes in their own homes. They become more present in their decision making and life choices, exemplifying for the next generation that leading with your core values creates profound transformations. The person's home, community, and world become more inclusive, welcoming, and peaceful environments for themselves and the people around them.

Why do we call this book *The Gift of Culture*? Because we want people to share it and join TCF Academy's mission: *To deliver $1 billion in value through 10,000 companies worldwide by 2030 so that companies thrive and their 1,000,000 associates love where they work and why they work so that they are fulfilled, loyal, and engaged.*

My hope is that companies all over the world will embrace this gift and shift toward valuing culture and improving the lives of people who work in enterprises of all kinds. People who are happy at work are more productive. Associates who feel valued and sense that they are making meaningful contributions to the world will give you more and stay with you longer. As a leader, if you believe people are your greatest asset, commit to it because investing in culture is investing in your people. Now that you have received *The Gift of Culture*, please pass it on to others so that they too don't work to live but rather live one fulfilling life.

Glossary

Actuator: An Actuator's role is to set Culture Fulfillment in motion and move your teams to action around a common goal: of uncovering and cultivating your organization's unique values and purpose

CoreVals™: a company's core values

CorePurpose™ a company's 'why' or reason for being

CoreTarget™: a target or measure (usually with a date) that quantifies the CorePurpose™ deliverable

CoreChart™: an infographic that combines a company's CoreVals™, CorePurpose™, and CoreTarget™

CoreScore™: a numeric measurement that indicates the degree to which employees and teams work in concert with CoreVals™

Core People Processes: the hiring, unhiring, and evaluating protocols based on CoreVals

Notice & Nominate™: a formalized scheme designed so employees can nominate one another for significant behaviors tied to company CoreVals

Catch & Correct™: a mechanism for handling behaviors that are out of line with values

Unhire™: decoupling from an employee

Culture Fulfillment™: the proven 9 Deeds in 90 Days that fulfills the best of what exists within a company/organization

Culture Czars*: team members who exemplify a company's CoreVals™ and are champions of the corporate culture

About the Author

Will Scott is passionate about creating environments where people thrive so that they can be the best that they can be. A culture devotee, Will has studied, researched, and adopted corporate culture strategies in several of his own companies, as well as helped hundreds of other businesses with their culture fulfillment. Each one has its own remarkable story.

Will leads workshops and speaks regularly on the subject of corporate culture using his proprietary 9-step process for taking organizations from simply having Core Values to truly having a Valued Culture. Author of *The Culture Fix: Bring your Culture Alive, Make it Thrive and Use it to Drive Performance* and host of The Culture Fix podcast, Will has set out to bring the gift of culture to 10,000 companies and their 1 million associates by 2030.

Active in the entrepreneurial community for more than two decades, he has led multi-chapter initiatives for the Entrepreneurs' Organization, served on several boards, and facilitated thousands of sessions as a business coach and strategic facilitator. With an MBA in international business from the University of Southern California, his career includes five start-ups, 2 exits, and several Inc. 5000 appearances before founding Culture Czars and The Culture Fix Academy.

Born in Zambia, Will is a European and naturalized US citizen who has lived in six countries and done business in more than 50. He has served in Her Majesty's Royal Marines, been active in the transformation of charitable organizations and not-for-profits, and is the proud father of Sam and Chloe. His favorite past times are yoga, meditation, triathlons, and spending time outdoors.

Products and Services

Culture Fulfillment is for you if you find yourself thinking:

- "My employees don't seem to care,"
- "I can't attract the best employees,"
- "I can't keep my best employees,"
- "My employees aren't accountable,"
- "I don't love the feeling of walking into my own office,"
- "We spend too much time talking about this problematic employee,"
- "There is too much drama and negative talk in the workplace,"
- "It seems like I have to make all of the decisions,"
- or "I don't know how to start and satisfactorily finish a difficult conversation."

Through speaking events, workshops, subscriptions, and a variety of implementations, TCF Academy Actuators can help you enhance your culture and help your team work more effectively together.

Speaking & Workshops

Through an interactive session with live demos, customized formats and durations to fit your organization's needs, an overview of the 9 Deeds in 90 Days, and a free copy of *The Culture Fix*, Will encourages your team to love where they work and why they work. Reach out to Will@ TheCultureFix.Academy.

The Culture Fix Academy

With a monthly subscription to The Culture Fix Academy, members join a supportive network and can access the full suite of tools—from the methodologies to the strategies, from surveys to case studies, from sample scripts to instructional videos that share the iterative process of Culture Fulfillment. Find out more at https://www.TheCultureFix.Academy

Additional Resources

Now that you've finished reading *The Gift of Culture*, I'd love to hear what you thought of it! Please share what you liked, disliked, or how this book has helped you and your company. You can do this by writing a review on *The Gift of Culture's* Amazon listing to help other readers find the best book for them. If you'd like to start a conversation, email me directly at Will@TheCultureFix.Academy.

Connect with Culture Czar Will Scott online via:
LinkedIn: https://www.linkedin.com/in/willjscott/

Twitter: https://twitter.com/WilljrScott

Facebook: https://www.facebook.com/CultureCzars/

Instagram: https://www.instagram.com/culture_czars/

Corporate Culture Blog
https://www.cultureczars.com/company-culture-ideas-blog

Culture Czars podcast series From Core Values To Valued Culture: https://www.cultureczars.com/vlogs

The Culture Fix Academy
www.TheCultureFix.Academy

Special Opportunity

Get your free download of Will Scott's *The Culture Fix*.

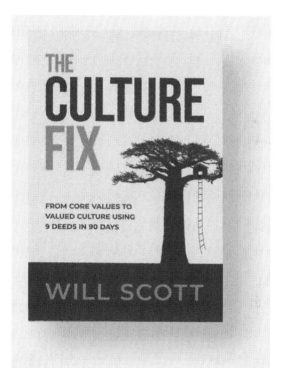

In just 90 days, Will Scott pulls apart 9 Deeds in order to bring your company's culture alive and transform it into a thriving, driven organism that goes beyond the four walls of your building. When you grow an atmosphere that your employees truly want to be in, you create a company that grows their ROI naturally. This book has the techniques to get you there.

Claim online at https://www.theculturefix.academy/enjoy-your-free-gift.

Made in United States
Orlando, FL
28 January 2023

29152835R00111